1

THE No 1
BOOK OF
NUMBERS

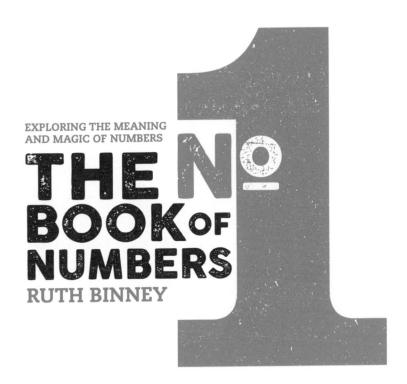

EXPLORING THE MEANING
AND MAGIC OF NUMBERS

THE N^o

BOOK OF

NUMBERS

RUTH BINNEY

RP

RYDON
PUBLISHING

A Rydon Publishing Book
35 The Quadrant
Hassocks
West Sussex
BN6 8BP
www.rydonpublishing.co.uk
www.rydonpublishing.com

First published by Rydon Publishing in 2018

A CIP catalogue record for this book is available from the British Library.

ISBN: 978-1-910821-17-6

Printed in Poland by BZ Graf

CONTENTS

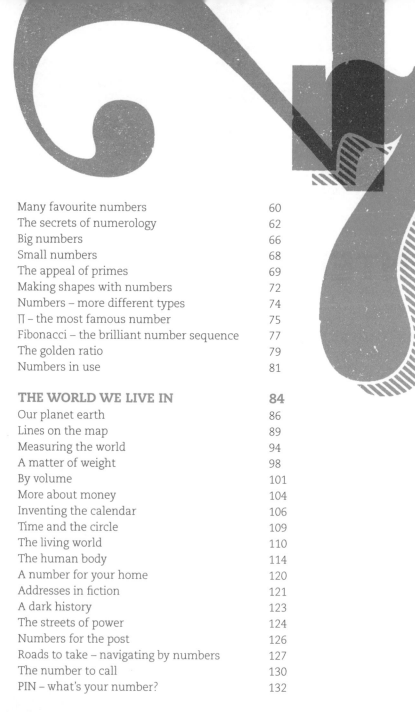

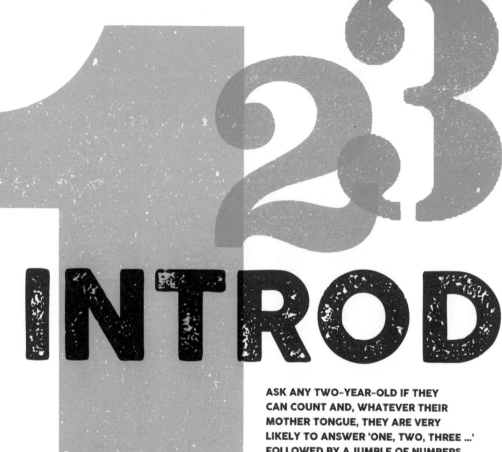

123

1NTROD

ASK ANY TWO-YEAR-OLD IF THEY CAN COUNT AND, WHATEVER THEIR MOTHER TONGUE, THEY ARE VERY LIKELY TO ANSWER 'ONE, TWO, THREE ...' FOLLOWED BY A JUMBLE OF NUMBERS SUCH AS 'FIVE, TEN, EIGHT ...'. THIS, SO RESEARCH ON NUMBER SUGGESTS, IS NOT SURPRISING, SINCE IT HAS BEEN DISCOVERED THAT EVEN NEWBORN BABIES HAVE AN INBUILT, HARD-WIRED RUDIMENTARY SENSE OF NUMBER, WHICH THEN DEVELOPS IN PARALLEL WITH THE LEARNING OF LANGUAGE. NUMBERS SO INFUSE OUR LIVES THAT AS ADULTS, MANY OF US HAVE LUCKY OR FAVOURITE NUMBERS AS WELL AS THOSE WE REGARD AS UNLUCKY. WHAT IS MORE, NUMBERS SUCH AS 22 (FROM THE BOOK TITLE), 66 (AS IN THE ROUTE) AND 64 (IN THE BEATLES' SONG) SPARK IMMEDIATE RECOGNITION.

Not only are numbers integral to our lives from the very start, but they were also crucial to the development of human societies, which began using counting and simple calculations to record amounts essential to their success such as quantities of grain, oil and other goods being traded. From these foundations numbers have been used over the centuries to quantify our world, from calendars, clocks and money systems to road, house and telephone numbers. As these have developed, so numbers have come to

1 to 10 – plus zero and the teens. Here too are lucky, unlucky and favourite numbers, the primes, the golden ratio and the fascinating Fibonacci series. Section two, The World We Live In explores the many ways in which numbers are used to measure our world, including time, money and temperature, and on the numbers that give it order right down to those associated with the way our bodies work and with our food, drinks and even beauty products. In the final section, For Our Leisure and Entertainment, the

acquire meanings far removed from pure mathematics. They can have religious or mythical significance, add crucial meaning to book, film or song title, define the quality of such precious items as gold and diamonds and act to standardize and record the sports and games we love.

Once I began researching and writing this book, it quickly became apparent that there was far more intruiging information than could possibly be included. So in many instances the choices I have made are purely personal. That said, I have attempted to create a wide-ranging treatment of the way in which numbers order and enrich our lives in three broad sections.

Section one, Numbers of Many Sorts, begins with the evolution of counting, followed by individual numbers from

focus is on poetry and proverbs, music, film, literature, popular sports and intriguing puzzles.

In creating this book I am hugely indebted to my partner Andrew Fawcett not only for his encouragement, but in helping to draft and check the more mathematical entries and those on sports. I have had the concept of this book in mind for many years so many thanks are due to my publisher Robert Ertle for bringing it to fruition and for the excellent input from my editor Verity Graves-Morris and designer Prudence Rogers.

My only wish now is that you enjoy reading The No1 Book of Numbers as much as I have loved writing it.

Ruth Binney
Yeovil, Somerset, 2018

NUMBERS OF MANY SORTS

Beyond the simple act of counting in any language, numbers have all manner of meanings. To the superstitious they can be lucky or unlucky – while to the mathematically minded they can be described in all kinds of ways such as odd or even, prime or perfect, square or triangular, abundant or amicable or simply large or small. What is indisputable, however, is that every number, including zero (which is technically not a number at all) has its own special attributes in a social as well as a scientific context. On a personal level, numbers take on special significance in the predictive practice of numerology, which relates to the ancient beliefs of the school of the Greek mathematician and philosopher Pythagoras.

In practical terms it is the numbers up to 12 that stand up to most scrutiny and here you will find everything from the origins of the expression 'One for all – all for one' to the many words for describing a pair to the significance of three in many religions. So many facts and ideas emerge, whether it is the five Olympic rings or the constant six-fold pattern of the snowflake, or the many meanings of seven – pure luck, wonders of the ancient world, deadly sins, Snow White's dwarves or 007 aka James Bond. And there are, of course, the nine lives of cats, the Ten Commandments and the traditional 12 members of a jury.

Just a few examples of the way numbers are put to use complete this part of the story, significantly with the law of averages, π (pi) and its use in measuring circles, and Fibonacci's number sequence, which relates remarkably closely to the golden mean, the perfect ratio able to imbue our world with features of perfect beauty.

NUMBERS AND COUNTING

FROM THE SIMPLEST BEGINNINGS THE ART OF COUNTING AND INVENTION OF NUMBERS – AND THE MANY WAYS IN WHICH THEY HAVE BEEN USED – HAVE SHAPED HUMAN LIVES THROUGHOUT THE AGES, DOWN TO TODAY'S WORLD OF MICROCHIPS AND MOBILE PHONES.

How numbers and counting began remains a mystery, but it is certain that without counting it would have been impossible for early families to share food supplies equally amongst themselves, or to count the numbers of arrowheads they might trade, for example, for a canoe. Of course the fingers – and toes – were perfect counting tools, as recorded in the Egyptians' *The Book of the Dead* written in the 16th century BCE. But imagine the excitement of the archaeologists working in Africa's Congo region who in 1960 unearthed the Ishango bone, a baboon's fibula around 20,000 years old and marked with a regular series of lines that do appear to represent a genuine means of counting.

Early systems

In the 3rd century BCE both the Egyptians and the Sumerians (from the southern region of Mesopotamia) developed systems for counting and calculating. For the Egyptians numbers were essential for reckoning the amounts of harvested grain on which taxes were collected, and for calculating the dimensions of their pyramids, temples, obelisks and other extraordinary structures. They counted in tens, and devised a series of hieroglyphs to denote specific numbers in which the symbol for 1 was a line, for 10 a rope and for 100 a curled rope, and 1,000 a lotus plant (see below).

A stone carving from 1500 BCE found in Karnac distinctly shows the number 276 depicted as 2 hundreds, 7 tens and 6 ones.

For the Sumerians, counting and simple arithmetic were means of organizing and keeping track of crops, livestock – and the people themselves – and involved the creation of clay tokens and, later, tablets on which equivalent wedge-shaped marks were made and verified with an official seal. Unlike the Egyptians the Sumerians devised a system based on 60 – surmised to be the number of digits on the hand multiplied by the number of constellations they recognized.

Like the Sumerians, the Babylonians also used a base 60 or sexagesimal system of counting and calculating, as we know from clay tablets made between 1800 and 1600 BCE. In this system the symbol for 60 and that for 1 are identical, but are easily distinguished by the position in which they are placed on the tablet. The reason that they favoured such a system was probably that 60 can be divided by 2, 3, 4, 5, 6, 10, 12, 15, 20 and 30 – and by

1   10   100   1,000

Egyptian numerals

𒁹 1	𒌋𒁹 11	𒌋𒌋𒁹 21	𒌍𒁹 31	𒐏𒁹 41	𒐐𒁹 51
𒐀 2	𒌋𒐀 12	𒌋𒌋𒐀 22	𒌍𒐀 32	𒐏𒐀 42	𒐐𒐀 52
𒐁 3	𒌋𒐁 13	𒌋𒌋𒐁 23	𒌍𒐁 33	𒐏𒐁 43	𒐐𒐁 53
𒐂 4	𒌋𒐂 14	𒌋𒌋𒐂 24	𒌍𒐂 34	𒐏𒐂 44	𒐐𒐂 54
𒐃 5	𒌋𒐃 15	𒌋𒌋𒐃 25	𒌍𒐃 35	𒐏𒐃 45	𒐐𒐃 55
𒐄 6	𒌋𒐄 16	𒌋𒌋𒐄 26	𒌍𒐄 36	𒐏𒐄 46	𒐐𒐄 56
𒐅 7	𒌋𒐅 17	𒌋𒌋𒐅 27	𒌍𒐅 37	𒐏𒐅 47	𒐐𒐅 57
𒐆 8	𒌋𒐆 18	𒌋𒌋𒐆 28	𒌍𒐆 38	𒐏𒐆 48	𒐐𒐆 58
𒐇 9	𒌋𒐇 19	𒌋𒌋𒐇 29	𒌍𒐇 39	𒐏𒐇 49	𒐐𒐇 59
𒌋 10	𒌋𒌋 20	𒌍 30	𒐏 40	𒐐 50	

Babylonian numerals

itself and one. As well as counting, the Babylonians certainly used fractions, approximation of π, and developed complex mathematics.

The Greeks and Romans
In ancient Greece mathematicians studied the work of the Babylonians but made the intellectual advance of regarding numbers as abstract as well as representing specific entities. Indeed they believed that numbers ruled the world. The mathematician Pythagoras (c. 570 –495 BCE) was intrigued by whole numbers and was the first to designate numbers as odd or even. For Pythagoras, who had studied in Egypt, the number one was the basis of the universe around which everything revolved and he and those of his school believed that behind numbers existed a fixed system of principles (see The Secrets off Numerology). Following Pythagoras Archimedes made great strides in mathematics, but his advances came to an abrupt end when he was killed by invading Romans in 212 BCE.

The Greeks used a base 10 system of counting, using alphabetic symbols to represent numbers from 1 to 9 and yet others for 10, 20 and so on, and for 100 up to 900. This has the great

MMXVIII

disadvantage, like so many of the ancient counting systems, that there was a finite supply of symbols. Before this system was established they employed one rather like the Romans, who used combinations of I, V, X, L, C, D and M to signify their numbers. Neither system made arithmetic simple, despite the fact that along with their empire the Romans spread their counting system, assisted by a form of abacus, across Europe.

The Hindu tradition and beyond

While advances were being made in the near East and Europe, counting and numbers were also being explored and developed in parallel in the far east. In India a system of symbols for the numbers one to nine – the foundation of the so-called Arabic numerals we use today – was devised as early as 500 BCE but from 3000 BCE units of weight graded 0.05, 0.1, 0.2, 0.5, 1, 2, 5, 10, 20, 50, 100, 200 and 500 were used in the development of trade and commerce.

It took much longer to develop a proper base 10 decimal system, which came properly to fruition with the 'invention' of zero in around AD 500 (see The story of zero).

It was Leonardo Pisano Bigollo, who became known as Fibonacci (see Fibonacci) who was instrumental in introducing Arabic numerals to Europe when, in 1202 he returned to Italy after travelling in Algeria with his merchant father. Only later did the 'new' system catch on, but its acceptance was spurred by the Catholic Reformation (known as the Counter-Reformation) of the mid-16th century which loosened the rules of trading and made Arabic-style calculation acceptable to the merchant classes.

In different languages

Although they may use base 10 in essence, counting systems are not always straightforward. Most languages use their own specific terms for the numbers between 10 and 20, the equivalents of our 11, 12 and then the teens. In French, for instance, multiples of 10 are simple up to 60 (*soixante*) but 70 is *soixante-dix* and 80 is *quatre-vingt* (four-twenty).

Danish is even more complex, demanding an understanding of fractions. Vitally, the number 50 or *halvtreds* (a shortened form of *halv tred sinds tyve*) means half third times 20 or 2½ x 20. This means that 70 is 3½ x 20 and 90 is 4½ x 20.

By contrast, Chinese has a very easy and regular system based on counting the number of tens and then adding the ones. So 11 is *shíyî*, which is 10 (*shí*) plus 1 (*yî*); 21 is *èrshíyi*, which is 2 (*èr*) times 10 (*shí*) plus 1 (*yî*) and so on.

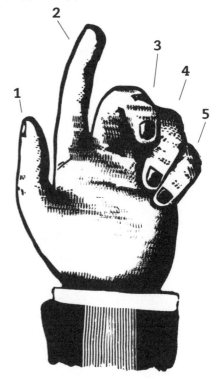

SOME COUNTING ODDITIES

The Oksapmin people of New Guinea use a base 27 system. Words for the numbers are body parts, starting with the thumb of one hand and ending on the thumb of the other, via fingers, arms, shoulders, head and face.

The Yoruba of West Africa have a base 20 system but for each 10 numbers advanced you add for the digits 1 to 4 and subtract for digits 5 to 9. So 13 is 10 + 3 while 18 is 20-2. This makes 77 (20 x 4) -3.

Traditional Welsh numbers are in base 20 with 15 used as a reference point so that 16 is 1 on 15, while 36 is 1 on 15 on 20, and so on.

In Mexico the Tzotzil-speaking Mayans count using fingers and toes but when these run out use those of the person next to them, making 37 the 'seventh toe of the second man'.

0	1	2	3	4
⊂⊃	•	••	•••	••••

5	6	7	8	9	10
—	•	••	•••	••••	—

Mayan numerals

ONE AND ZERO – THE BINARY SYSTEM

WITHOUT THE BINARY NUMBER SYSTEM OF CALCULATION IT IS EXTREMELY UNLIKELY THAT THIS BOOK COULD HAVE BEEN TYPED ON A COMPUTER. ALTHOUGH IT IS SAID TO HAVE BEEN INVENTED BY THE CHINESE, AND TO HAVE BEEN USED IN ANCIENT EGYPT AND INDIA, WE REALLY OWE BINARY TO THE GERMAN MATHEMATICIAN GOTTFRIED LEIBNIZ (1646–1716) WHO DOCUMENTED IT IN HIS ARTICLE *EXPLICATION DE L'ARITHMÉTIQUE BINAIRE* OF 1679.

In his ponderings about mathematics, philosophy and religion, which included study of the *I Ching*, the Chinese book of divination, dating to the 9th century BCE, and based on the duality of yin and yang, the Sinophile Leibnitz came to associate the number 1 with God and 0 with nothingness. From these two alone, he surmised, every other number could be created. He was also fascinated by the fact that the hexagrams depicted in the *I Ching* corresponded to binary numbers ranging from 0 to 111111.

By 1725 the French silk maker Basil Bouchon had developed a roll of paper by which he could control his looms. The warp threads on the machine were set in motion, or not, depending on whether or not a space on the paper contained a punched hole. The paper rolls were superseded by punched cards, and it was such cards that Charles Babbage used in his Analytical Engine first described in 1837.

Other key characters in the development of binary included the British mathematician George Boole whose 1854 paper on logic was implemented in 1937 by the American mathematician and cryptographer Claude Shannon. In the same year George Sibbitz of the Bell Laboratories invented a computer on his kitchen table (he named it Model K), which worked using binary addition.

How binary works
In the binary system each digit represents a power of 2, not one of 10 as we are used to in the decimal system. So 101 represents 2×2 (that is 1 unit and no 2s), plus one unit, making a total of 4 + 1 = 5. This table shows how it works:

PRACTICALITIES OF BINARY

To avoid confusion with decimal numbers binary are pronounced in a different way. So 4 is voiced as one-zero-zero and 5 as one-zero-one.

Binary notation is now commonly used on appliance and switches with 1 representing 'on' and 0 as 'off'.

DECIMAL	BINARY
0	0
1	1
2	10
3	11
4	100
5	101
6	110
7	111
8	1000

1 – THE NUMBER OF UNITY

ONE IS ONE AND ALL ALONE AND EVER MORE SHALL BE SO…. FROM THE TRADITIONAL SONG 'GREEN GROW THE RUSHES-O'.

Strange as it may seem, the ancient Greeks did not regard one as a number at all. Indeed Pythagoras called it 'No Number' adding that '… there is neither first nor last, for all is one…'. The ancients also believed that one was not only indivisible but the number from which all other numbers arose for, as Euclid maintained, a number exists only as an aggregate of various units. This view was strengthened by the ancients' association of one with the Deity – a supernatural, indivisible being. Such a belief was also held by the Romans.

Mathematically, the Greeks generally regarded one as being both odd and even (Pythagoras deemed it to be odd), and although they were wrong in this they were correct in noting that it is the only number that produces less by multiplication than by addition simply because any number multiplied by one remains the same. However fractions did not exist for them and anything less than one, such as ⅔ was regarded as a new number in its own right.

Being number one

To be first – or number one – is what people in almost every field of life dream of achieving. The Romans called it *primus inter pares*, or 'first among equals', and used it as an honorary title for the member of the senate given the privilege of speaking first in any debate. Following the fall of the Republic, however, they simply called themselves *princeps*. In modern times, the expression was employed by former MP Jeffrey Archer in his 1984 novel charting the lives of two men vying to be Prime Minister. On the non-fiction shelves you can find *One-upmanship*, the 1952 best-selling humorous workplace guide by Stephen Potter.

Chart toppers

In the world of pop music singles charts were first compiled in 1952. The first ever number one, announced on November 14 of that year, was 'Here in my Heart' by Al Martino which stayed at number one for nine weeks. In the UK, Elvis Presley holds the record for most number one singles with 20. Most weeks at number one was Frankie Laine with 'I Believe' in 1953. In the USA The Beatles top the list with 20 number one singles. To date the record for weeks at number one is 16, held by Mariah Carey and Boyz II Men's 'One Sweet Day', in 1995–96.

EXPRESSIONS OF ONE

Of the many ways of expressing one-ness these are among the most used:

One for all – all for One (*Unus pro omnibus, omnes pro uno*) – the traditional motto of Switzerland since 1902. Inverted to 'All for one and one for all' it is renowned as the watchword of the Three Musketeers in Alexandre Dumas' novel of 1844 (see Books with numbers).

'I believe in One God …' – the opening words of the Apostle's Creed.

To be one flesh – to be united in marriage.

To keep oneself to oneself – to be alone.

Every football fan thinks that their team is the best, a sentiment often expressed in song, as is loudly rendered at Selhurst Park, home of Crystal Palace: 'Stand in the rain and stand in the sun/We are South London's number one.'

ONE EYED CREATURES

Single-eyed mythological beings come in many bizarre forms and have an extremely ancient history.

According to the Greek author Homer, a race of cave-dwelling giants existed, each with a single eye in the middle of the forehead. Chief of these Cyclopes was Polyphemus, who liked to eat his humans raw. To the poet Hesiod the Cyclopes were three in number and godlike in nature, commanding power over the sun, lightning and thunder.

Similar tales exist in other cultures. In eastern European mythology, one-eyed giants also live in caves while in Ireland the Surly One of Lachiann guards the sacred quicken tree, which is home to powerful spirits. In Yorkshire a one-eyed giant grinds up his victims and bakes them in bread. The roots of these tales stretch back, it has been discovered, to the early Stone Age and may even be depicted in a bizarre sculpture found in the cave of the Trois-Frères in southern France.

EQUALLY BIZARRE

Other one-eyed creatures include:

• **Kasa-obake** – the mythical ghost of Japanese folklore often believed to be incarnated from old umbrellas.

• **Likho** – in Slavic mythology, the embodiment of the extremes of both evil and ill fortune, who can appear as a skinny old woman or a male goblin.

• **Mapinguari** – a stinking giant sloth-like creature from the rainforests of Brazil and Bolivia with lizard-like skin and a second mouth on its abdomen.

• **Snallygaster** – a dragon-like creature, part bird, part reptile, believed to live in the hills around central Maryland and Washington DC.

2 – THE DUALITY

THE ANIMALS WENT IN TWO BY TWO....
(NURSERY RHYME)

The Duad, as it was known to Pythagoras and his school, is the number that stands for opposites – day and night, good and evil, love and hate. This duality meant that both sides of an argument should always be heard, and so also represents balance, harmony and justice. Despite adhering to these high values the ancient Greeks found the number two troubling because it has a beginning and an end but no 'centre'. It therefore simultaneously represented diversity and disorder which, they believed, underlaid strife and possibly even evil.

Two is the first even number, the first prime and the only prime that is an even number. Also, any number multiplied by 2, say $14 \times 2 = 28$ is the same as that number added to itself: $14 + 14 = 28$. This property was also puzzling.

The significance of two in the Old Testament is illustrated by the pairs of animals that Noah took into his Ark on God's instruction, and the twin tablets on which Moses received the Ten Commandments. To this day Jewish families place two loaves of challah on the table at each Friday Shabbat meal in memory of the two helpings of manna that fell from the heavens during the days of exile in the desert. In the popular carol 'two turtle doves' are the gift on the second day of Christmas.

The language of two

To be designated a number two is to be second in command, or importance, but there are a whole host of words and expressions that describe the different nature of two.

Pair – any combination of two things or people, whether closely or loosely connected.

Duo – very often a pair of performers, who together might play a duet.

Dual – describes a pairing. Dualism is a philosophical system in which everything that exists is categorized into one of two principles such as good and evil.

Duality – a pairing, often of opposites such as ying and yang.

Dyad – two individuals regarded as a pair such as mother and daughter. Also sets of two things.

Couple – also a pairing, often of people but also used in mechanics and physics.

Double – used in arithmetic to indicate multiplication by two. To be someone's double is to be their spitting image. The concept can be expressed in anything from a double chin to a double-edged

THE TWO HEADER

The Roman god Janus is famous for having two faces in the same head, one pointing in each direction. Many scholars think he was the god of night and day but also of beginnings and endings, since he looks to both the past and the future. Janus worship was instigated by Romulus, founder of Rome with his twin Remus, and his temple was sited at the northern edge of the Forum. The month of January was named for and dedicated to him.

sword that can cut on either edge, either literally or metaphorically.

Twin – a 'birth condition' that can pair you with a sibling of the same genetic make up or one only as similar as any other brother or sister. Also used for closely placed objects, most famously New York's Twin Towers.

Tandem – a 'bicycle made for two' in the words of the song 'Daisy, Daisy'. Togetherness, however played out, may well be in tandem.

Brace – a pair, most often applied to game birds such as pheasant or partridge.

Binary – involving two things, notably twinned stars or other astronomical bodies, but specifically a means of counting and calculation.

3 – THE TRINITY OF PERFECTION

I ALMOST WISH WE WERE BUTTERFLIES AND LIV'D BUT THREE SUMMER DAYS – THREE SUCH DAYS WITH YOU I COULD FILL WITH MORE DELIGHT THAN FIFTY COMMON YEARS COULD EVER CONTAIN.
THE POET JOHN KEATS IN A LETTER TO FANNY BRAWNE.

Three was, to the Pythagoreans, the union between unity and diversity representing perfect harmony. This was not least because they believed in three worlds – the Inferior, the Superior and the Supreme. In a similar way, adherents of the philosophers Plato and Socrates revered the number because of its association with the three principles of Matter, Idea and God, and with the triple virtues of justice, prudence and fortitude.

The Triad

The number three, or the Triad, had many other meanings and connotations in the ancient world. Having a beginning, middle and an end, and because it increased more when multiplied by itself than when added (nine compared with six) it was regarded as the first 'real' or 'true' number. Three was also linked to the triangle, which has both three edges and three vertices (points). It is the second prime number and the first odd one and, arithmetically, any number can be divided by three only if the sum of its digits can be divided by three exactly – for example 372 = 124/3. Scientifically there are three states of matter – solid, liquid and gas – and, simplistically, three states of time – past, present and future. And, if we set aside the fourth dimension of time itself, the world can be measured in the three dimensions of length, depth and breadth.

A symbolic number

Thinking of things in threes has been common down the centuries and forms a central tenet of both mythology and religion. For the Egyptians, three epitomized plurality, and was represented by three vertical lines (I I I). The Greeks believed that there were three Graces, Fates and Furies. The Nine Muses (see The Nine Muses) were three times three. Norse mythology recognized three races of giants representing mountains, frost and fire and the heart of the giant Hrungir was a stone triangle. Yggdrasil, their 'world tree' has three roots which join nine worlds. The symbol of three interlocked triangles, the Valknut, was used by the Vikings as a symbol for those slain in conflict and is associated with the Norse god Odin. For the Chinese, three is a lucky number which has long signified the three key stages in human life, namely birth, marriage and death.

Valknut

Religious significance

To Christians, the Trinity of Father, Son and Holy Spirit is central to belief. In a comparable way, Hindus revere the Trumurti which represents the roles of three gods Brahms (creation), Vishnu (preservation) and Shiva (destruction). Depicted in a three-faced figure the trio are believed to be individual incarnations of a single deity. As a commitment to their faith, Buddhists take refuge in the Three Jewels or Triple Gem, which are the Buddah, the prime source of authority and inspiration, the Dhamma, the teachings of the Buddah, and the Sanga, which is the monastic community of celibate monks and nuns that the Buddha founded.

The number three occurs frequently in religious texts and practices. In Judaism there are three patriarchs (Abraham, Isaac and Jacob); a Beth din – a Rabbinical court of justice – consists of 3 members; 3 daily prayers are said; and 3 matzos set on the Seder table at Passover. In Christianity – the Magi brought the infant Jesus 3 gifts; the Devil tempted Jesus 3 times; Peter denied Jesus 3 times; and Jesus rose from the dead on the third day. In Zoroastrianism there are three ethical principles of good or Humata – thinking, speaking and acting. The modern pagan tradition of Wicca acknowledges the triple Goddess represented by three phases of the moon.

☆

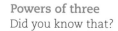

Powers of three
Did you know that?

■ A circle can be drawn through any three points not placed in a straight line.

■ An oath is traditionally repeated three times.

■ With only three primary colours – red, yellow and blue – you can mix most other colours.

■ The number three features in many folktales – think three bears, three little pigs and the three billy goats gruff.

■ According to British Prime Minister Benjamin Disraeli (1804–81) there are three types of untruth – lies, damned lies and statistics.

■ The shamrock or three-leaved clover is the symbol of Ireland.

■ In Russia a *troika* can be a triplet, a sledge pulled by three horses, or a dance made up of groups of three. It is also a committee consisting of three members and under Stalin was used in speedy prosecutions of political criminals.

■ To get your point – or joke – over to best effect follow the example of the ancient Greeks whose tricolon or 'rule of three' was essential to their rhetoric. Grouped in threes your message is sure to make an impact.

■ Three golden balls is the old sign for a pawnbroker.

The journey of the Magi

THE THREE GRACES

To the Greeks the Charites or Graces were the personification of charm and loveliness, creativity and fertility. Often depicted as attendants of Aphrodite, the goddess of beauty, they were Aglaea meaning splendour, Euphrosyne meaning Mirth, and Thalia whose name translates to good cheer. They are thought to epitomize the Greek ideal of the balance between restraint and licentious behaviour and were worshipped in Athens and many other places.

Known to the Romans as the Graces, and originally depicted clothed, later representations, such as the 1st century fresco found in Pompeii, shows them naked, linked in a circle as gracious as their name suggests.

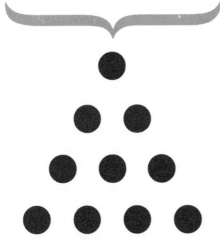

The sacred tetraktys symbol

4 – TRUTH AND JUSTICE

GOOD AUTHORS TOO/WHO ONCE USED BETTER WORDS/NOW ONLY USE FOUR-LETTER WORDS – COLE PORTER FROM HIS 1934 MUSICAL *ANYTHING GOES.*

Also known to the ancient Greeks as the Tetrad, four was seen as the number of truth, stability and justice. This regard was expressed by the Pythagoreans in the name even-even which they gave to any number that could be divided by four, and both four and eight were particularly revered. They also believed the world to be composed of earth, air, fire and water – the four elements considered to be the source of everything.

The significance of four was even more enhanced when linked to the four seasons of the year, four points of the compass – originally the four corners of the world – and four phases of the moon. The temperament of each person was thought to be one of four categories or humours each associated with a season: blood (spring); yellow bile (summer); black bile (autumn); and phlegm (winter).

The Pythagoreans not only believed that the soul existed in four parts (mind, opinion, science and sense) but also devised a sacred symbol, the tetraktys representing the numbers 1 to 4 arranged in a triangle (see The secrets of Numerology).

Dimensions and patterns

Four is significant when it comes to shape. We think of solid objects having four dimensions of length breadth, depth and height and easily recognize that a square has four sides and four points (vertices). The tetrahedron, the simplest so-called Platonic solid, which has faces made up of four triangles also has four vertices (see 5 – The number of nature). Space-time, the fourth dimension, as proposed by Albert Einstein in his special theory of relativity in 1905, expressed the concept that the three dimensions of space and the one dimension of time are fused into a single continuum.

Making maps

Four is a key number when it comes to creating maps. In 1852, basing his conclusions simply on 'common knowledge', the English mathematician and botanist Francis Guthrie was the first to suggest that any map – not just the one of England's counties he used as his template – could be coloured using only four colours. Proof of his theory was elusive, however, and only in 1976 did the US mathematicians Kenneth Appel and Wolfgang Haken manage to solve it, with the help of a computer processing data from thousands of examples.

Number in belief

The Pythagoreans commonly referred to God as the Tetrad because the name of Zeus, whom they believed to rule heaven and earth, had four letters (it was a tetragrammaton). In a religious context four has a great many connotations. In Judaism there

are four matriarchs, Sarah, Rebekah, Rachel and Leah and four expressions of redemption are said at Passover. Christians base their beliefs on the four gospels of Matthew, Mark, Luke and John while the agents of utter destruction, the Four Horsemen of the Apocalypse, appear in the Book of Revelation.

Hindu knowledge is contained in four Vedas – Rigveda, Samaveda, Yajurveda and Atharvaveda and Muslims honour four sacred months. Buddhists adhere to the Four Noble Truths of suffering (Dukkha), the cause of suffering (Samudaya), the cessation of suffering (Nirodha) and the path that leads to the cessation of suffering (Magga), and believe in four stages of enlightenment.

THE MANY SIDES OF FOUR

Four appears in our lives in many forms and contexts:

The four-leaved clover is believed to bring luck to the finder.

Tetraphobia, a fear of the number four, is common in East Asia, especially China, Japan and Taiwan, because it sounds very similar to the word for death.

The sub four-minute mile was run for the first time by Briton Roger Bannister on 6 May 1954 when he clocked 3 minutes 59.4 seconds at the Iffley Road track in Oxford.

Four thieves vinegar was a once-secret herbal mix said to have been drunk by thieves in France at the time of the Black Death. Also known as Marseilles vinegar it contained, among other things, wormwood, horehound, rosemary, angelica and cloves.

A four-letter word is a euphemism for a swear word.

The Fourth Estate is the press, a name coined by Edmund Burke, the 18th-century Irish statesman and philosopher.

The Fourth of July is America's Independence Day.

A quadrangle is a four-sided college courtyard, often with a lawn in the middle.

A quad is one of quadruplets, four babies delivered together.

A quadrille is both a card game for four players and a fiendishly difficult square dance.

Quarter days are the four days in the year when, traditionally, tenancies were renewed – or not. They fell on 25 March (Lady Day); 24 June (Midsummer Day); 29 September (Michaelmas Day) and 25 December (Christmas Day).

5 – THE NUMBER OF NATURE

The pentacle, a five-pointed star, is an ancient symbol of human kind, its points representing our four limbs and our head. And of course, we have five fingers and five toes on each limb. Not only are there five senses, but the sense of taste can detect five basic 'flavours' (see The human body). Five is also a recurrent number in the natural world, from the five arms of a starfish to the five petals of a wild rose.

Pentacle

Symbols and shapes

To ancient philosophers five was a symbol of health, but also of marriage and procreation, because it was the union of two, the first female number, and three the first male one. The Romans marked this significance by lighting five tapers at a marriage ceremony. Mathematically, the Pythagoreans called five the number of nature because when multiplied by itself the resulting number always ends in a five. This property, known as automorphism was, they believed, inherently self-destructive. They also associated it with Ether, or quintessence, their fifth element, which they believed to be critical in star formation.

In geometry, five is the smallest possible value of the hypotenuse in a right-angled triangle, with the other sides being three and four. And such a triangle is the only one whose area is exactly half its perimeter. A polygon with five sides is a pentagon. Five is also the total of the Platonic or regular solids (see right), which are named for the Greek philosopher Plato. In his dialogue entitled the *Timaeus* he put forward the hypothesis that all the elements of which the world was believed to be constructed (earth, air, fire, water and the ether) were composed of these five solids, each of which can be thought of as the meeting of triangles, squares or pentagons, with all the sides being identical (see opposite).

In different contexts

To the ancient Egyptians, the pentagram represented the afterlife and they believed that the god Thoth had added five days to the year by winning moonlight in a bet. For the Chinese, like the Greeks, five was associated with the world's elements – water, fire, earth, wood and metal. To afford protection against the Evil Eye, peoples of the Middle East have long carried a Hamsa Hand, a form of amulet bearing the image of a hand with two symmetrical thumbs on either side of three fingers. In the Jewish tradition this is often known as the Hand of Miriam (sister of Moses and Aaron) or Khamsa, and may also signify the five books of the Torah: Genesis, Exodus, Leviticus, Numbers and Deuteronomy.

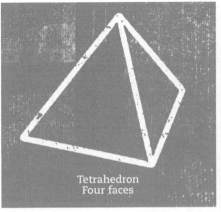

Tetrahedron
Four faces

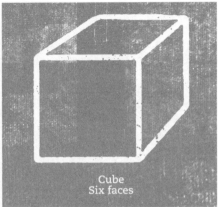

Cube
Six faces

The Platonic solids

Also in a religious context, devout Moslems pray five times each day but follow the Five Pillars of Islam which are faith, prayer, charity, fasting and pilgrimage to Mecca. For Sikhs there exist five sacred symbols of faith, all beginning with the letter k: *kesh* (uncut hair), *kangha* (the comb), *kara* (the steel bracelet), *kachhehra* (the soldier's shorts) and *kirpan* (the sword). For Christians five is the number of pebbles used by David to kill Goliath and the wounds suffered by Christ at his crucifixion.

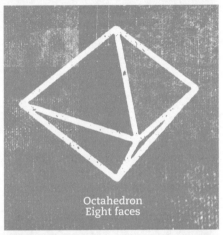

Octahedron
Eight faces

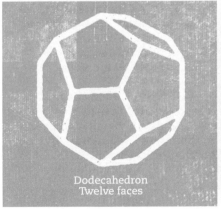

Dodecahedron
Twelve faces

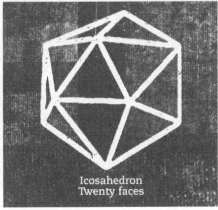

Icosahedron
Twenty faces

SIGNS, SYMBOLS AND SAYINGS

The five-petalled Luther Rose or Seal was designed in 1530 as a symbol of his movement for the German protestant reformer Martin Luther.

The symbol of the Olympic Movement is five interlocking rings, representing these continents – Europe (blue), Asia (yellow), Africa, (black), Oceania (green) and the Americas (red).

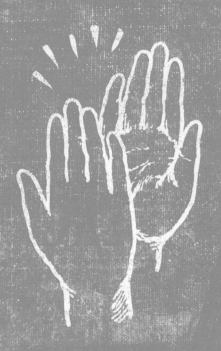

A five-finger exercise on the piano is a challenge involving all the fingers of one or both hands.

A high five is a celebration of success in which two people raise and join their hands ... but a bunch of fives is a closed fist ready to strike a blow.

In basketball only five players of a team are allowed on the court at any time.

The Fifth Amendment is part of the United States Constitution. It protects individuals outside the military from being compelled to bear witness against themselves.

Fifth Avenue is the New York street home to the world's top fashion outlets.

A fifth column consists of traitors working for an enemy in their own country.

The fifth of November is the day in 1605 when Guy Fawkes and his compatriots attempted to blow up London's Houses of Parliament and is still celebrated annually with bonfires and fireworks.

'Five Go Mad in Dorset', a parody of Enid Blyton's *Famous Five* (see Books with numbers), was aired on Channel 4's inaugural night on 2 November 1982.

6 – WITHOUT A FAULT

SOMETIMES I'VE BELIEVED AS MANY AS SIX IMPOSSIBLE THINGS BEFORE BREAKFAST.' LEWIS CARROLL, AUTHOR OF ALICE'S ADVENTURES IN WONDERLAND (1865).

In a perfect number, each of the numbers by which it can be divided add up to the number itself. Six is the first of these and was known to Pythagoras and his followers, being the sum of 1, 2 and 3. What is more, when the number itself is included, making a total of 12, then dividing by 2 gives the original number. To the ancient Greeks this property was a rarity and apart from 6 the only other perfect numbers that they recognized were 28, 496 and 8,128 (to types of numbers).

Writing in praise of the number's perfection, St Augustine (AD 354–430) wrote in *The City of God* that: 'Six is a number perfect in itself, not because God created all things in six days; rather, the contrary is true. God created all things in six days because the number is perfect.' Geometrically, a hexagon is a balanced, six-sided figure and six has long been regarded as a number of harmony, completion and justice. Two intersecting triangles compose a six-pointed star, which to the Pythagoreans symbolized the union of spirit and matter, male and female making it, like five, a number associated with marriage.

Star of David

Chance and fate

Known also as the Star of David, the six-pointed star was, in medieval times, incorporated into the Seal of Solomon, a signet ring believed to have been owned by the eponymous king of Israel. Thought to be possessed of magical powers that could ward off evil, the seal subsequently found its way into a variety of occult movements. The star was used to chilling and murderous effect by the Third Reich to mark out Jewish people and properties.

The cube, which we also know in the form of a dice or die, is a regular solid with six sides.

MUCH MARRIED

Henry VIII, who reigned England from 28 June 1491 to 28 January 1547, remains notorious for having wed six wives: Catherine of Aragon, Anne Boleyn, Jane Seymour, Anne of Cleves, Catherine Howard and Catherine Parr. Their fates can easily be remembered with the rhyme: 'Divorced, beheaded, died/ Divorced, beheaded, survived'.

Made originally from animal bones, its origins are obscure, but archaeologists have discovered remains of dice dating to around 2500 BCE in Iran and in Sumerian graves in Asia of a similar vintage. To the ancient Greeks, the best throw was a triple six, a result deemed to bring good luck (see Throwing dice).

Six degrees of separation is the concept that everyone on earth is connected by six or fewer links. The theory was originally proposed in 1929 by the Hungarian author Karinthy Frigyes in his short story *Láncszemek* (*Chains*). His theory has since had a significant influence on social networking. It was also the inspiration for the 1990 play and popular 1993 film by Irish-American John Guare.

THE SHADES OF SIX

To be hit for six is to be dealt a body blow – because a six is the highest scoring shot in cricket in which the ball crosses the boundary without hitting the ground.

To be at sixes and sevens is to be undecided.

In the days of corporal punishment six of the best was a euphemism for strokes of the cane administered by a schoolteacher.

The Six Nations is the annual rugby union tournament played by England, Scotland, Wales, Ireland, France and Italy.

Our sixth sense is our intuition or, possibly, supernatural power of prediction.

In ice hockey a team may have a maximum of six players on the ice at any time.

A 'six pack' can be a group of six bottles or cans of drink sold together or the well-developed abdominal muscles produced by working out.

Because it sounds similar to the word luck, the Chinese regard six as a lucky number, especially in business.

In Norse mythology the superbly strong leash used to tame the dreaded Fenrir wolf consisted of six items: the sound of a cat walking, a woman's beard, a mountain's roots, a bear's sinews, a fish's breath and a bird's spit.

SIX AND THE SNOWFLAKE

THEY COME IN A MULTITUDE OF STUNNINGLY BEAUTIFUL SHAPES AND SIZES, FROM THE SIMPLE TO THE HIGHLY COMPLEX, AND EVERY SNOWFLAKE THAT FALLS HAS ITS OWN INDIVIDUAL IDENTITY. WHAT ALMOST ALL SNOWFLAKES SHARE IS THE PROPERTY OF BEING SIX SIDED.

High in the sky, where temperatures are low, it takes the presence of a speck of dust or debris – or perhaps a bacterium – to trigger snowflake formation. As the snowflake forms, supercooled water molecules freeze and bond together as crystals. At first they form four-sided pyramidal shapes, then as they gradually come closer together crystallize into hexagons.

As each snowflake enlarges its six 'arms' or dendrites enlarge according to the precise microclimate that surrounds it. When the flakes finally become heavy enough to fall to the ground the changes in air temperature and humidity alter

SNOWY LANGUAGE

In mid 19th century Missouri, 'snowflake' was used to describe someone who was opposed to the abolition of slavery. In modern parlance a snowflake is a derogatory term for someone who is too full of themselves and who is adjudged liable to 'melt' when the going gets tough.

their structure yet again, leading to the wonderfully complex patterns visible when snowflakes are observed under the microscope. The 'ideal' snowflake is perfectly symmetrical but in fact such perfection occurs rarely in nature. Also rare is the 12-sided snowflake, a variation on the six-sided form.

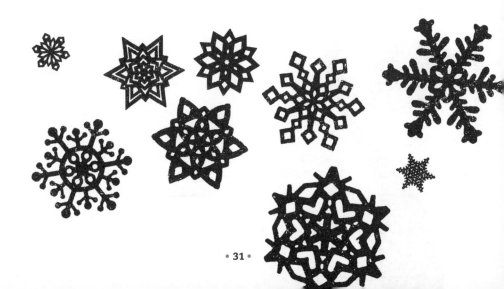

7 – THE SYMBOL OF FORTUNE

ONE MAN IN HIS TIME PLAYS MANY PARTS, HIS ACTS BEING SEVEN AGES.
WILLIAM SHAKESPEARE'S *AS YOU LIKE IT.*

From the seven colours of the rainbow to Snow White's Seven Dwarfs, and from the seven deadly sins to the days of the week, the number seven has had a huge presence in human lives since the earliest times. We have seven continents and travel the world on its seven oceans. Seven is a number of perfection and fortune, of security, rest and safety. For many seven is the luckiest number (see Lucky – and unlucky – numbers), but to break a mirror will, say the superstitious, bring seven years of bad luck.

Mathematically, seven is the fourth prime number. The Pythagoreans, who called it the Septad, regarded it as a perfect number comprising three, the spirit (composed of father, mother and son) and four, which is the root of all things earthly. For them seven was the number that governed the rhythm of life. Seven was also the symbol of perfection and completeness – and for the Egyptians was a 'God number', not least because seven years marked the end of the country's legendary famine that ended when the Nile flood rose to a level of seven cubits.

In Christian belief

Seven has significance in belief systems and rituals worldwide. The Old Testament recounts the seven days of creation – the seventh being the day of rest – and the Pharaoh's dream of the seven years' famine following seven years of plenty. In the New Testament, seven loaves were used (with two fishes) to feed the multitude and in the Book of Revelation are found Seven Spirits of God and Seven Churches. Here are also included seven each of: golden lampstands, stars, torches of fire, seals, angels and trumpets, last plagues, golden bowls, thunders, horns and eyes, diadems and kings.

Both sins and virtues come in sevens in Christian practice. The seven deadly sins are lust, gluttony, greed, sloth, wrath, envy and pride. By contrast the seven virtues are chastity, temperance, charity, diligence, kindness, patience and humility.

In other faiths

In the Hindu tradition there are seven Chakras or centres within the body through which energy flows and relate to the root (support), sacrum, solar plexus, heart, throat, the third eye (essentially the mind) and the crown (the top of the head). At Hindu weddings the bride and groom will circle the holy fire seven times while at a Jewish wedding seven blessings are recited under the traditional canopy, the *chuppah*. In Islam seven is significant as the number of doors to hell as well as the number of heavens and hells.

In Japanese folklore, seven is the number of the lucky gods who sail aboard the treasure ship *Takarabune*. They are believed to make an appearance every New Year and bring gifts to those deemed worthy to receive them. For good children a welcome New Year gift is an envelope containing money and decorated with an image of the ship. On 7 January each year the Japanese celebrate the festival of Seven Herbs (*Nanakusa no sekku*) when, for health and longevity, they eat a herb-flavoured rice porridge.

In the Bahá'I faith believers set out to travel Seven Valleys (or Cities), which takes their souls on a journey of enlightenment from the 'abode of dust' to the 'heavenly homeland'. Each aim for a different goal:

1. The Valley of Search
2. The Valley of Love
3. The Valley of Knowledge
4. The Valley of Unity
5. The Valley of Contentment
6. The Valley of Wonderment
7. The Valley of True Poverty and Absolute Nothingness

On the flag

For the Cherokee of North America, seven is the most sacred number and also represented the seven sacred ceremonies held between March and November and timed according to the moon's phases. Six of these traditionally took place each year, the seventh being saved for the seventh year.

The Cherokee had two flags each featuring the seven stars of the Plough or Big Dipper; the peace flag had red stars on a white background while on the war flag the colours were reversed. The Cherokee have an additional flag bearing a central seal motif surrounded by seven yellow seven-pointed stars representing the seven Cherokee clans. An additional black star in the top right-hand corner symbolizes those who lost their lives in the Trail of Tears – the forced removal of tribes from the southeastern United States initiated by president Andrew Jackson in 1831.

The shape of seven

A figure with seven sides is known as a heptagon while the universal symbol for the so-called 'Seed of Life', used iconically in many eastern religions and related to the Chakras, consists of seven overlapping circles, the innermost of which represents a day of rest. The circles are thought to mirror our chakras, the colours of the rainbow and even musical scales.

In solid form the British 50 pence piece is a heptagon as is the puzzle known as a tangram, which probably originated in China in the 7th century. In it seven flat shapes or tans, in different colours, and which fit exactly into a square, are used in a myriad of puzzles to create different shapes.

The Seed of Life

The power of seven

Facts and phenomena involving the number seven come in many forms:

- The number 999,999 when divided by 7 comes to exactly 142,857.

- When devising a code number for James Bond Ian Fleming concluded that only 007 had the right ring to it.

- In 2000 the Clay Mathematics Institute at Oxford University stated seven Millennium Prize problems. To date, only one of these has been solved.

- In music there are seven notes on the diatonic scale.

- The system of Roman numerals has seven letters: I, V, X, L, C, D and M.

- Rome is said to have seven hills, the first of which, the Palatine Hill, is believed to be where Romulus founded the city in 753 BCE.

- It is deemed extraordinarily lucky to be born the seventh son of the seventh son.

- The name of north London's Seven Sisters district comes from seven elm trees that were once planted around an area known as Page Green.

- Mahama Ghandi comprised a list of Seven Blunders of the World which he believed were the root of violence: wealth without work; pleasure without conscience; knowledge without character; commerce without morality; science without humanity; religion without sacrifice; and politics without principle.

LONG-LOVED STORY

Snow White came to life in the tales of the Brothers Grimm first published in German in 1812. In the original story the dwarfs did not have names; the first names ascribed to them were given in a Broadway play which opened on 31 October 1912, but they are not ones that we would recognize today: Blick (the eldest), Flick, Glick, Snick, Plick, Whick and Quee (the youngest but already 99 years old).

In 1916, a film adaptation of the play – a silent movie starring Marguerite Clark and Creighton Hale – was seen one day by the 15-year-old Walt Disney who in 1937 turned it into his first full length animated film with the dwarfs renamed as we know and love them today: Bashful, Doc, Dopey, Grumpy, Happy, Sleepy and Sneezy.

Snow White
and the Seven Dwarfs

THE SEVEN WONDERS OF THE WORLD

MAKING LISTS WAS A FAVOURITE OCCUPATION OF THE ANCIENT GREEKS. MOST FAMOUS OF ALL WERE THEIR SEVEN WONDERS OF THE WORLD – SPLENDID EDIFICES DEEMED WORTHY OF EMULATION.

The buildings in the list, known as 'themata' or 'things to be seen', were exclusively Greek, but in the early 3rd century BCE foreign ones were also included, reflecting the way that conquest had opened the world up to travellers. The well-accepted list of Antipater of Sidon, recorded in *Anthologia Palatina* (a collection of poetry of around 140 BCE) was headed by the walls of Babylon, but this was later replaced with the Lighthouse of Alexandria.

The Great Pyramid of Giza, Egypt

The only ancient wonder surviving today, and the oldest on the list, was constructed between 2584 and 2561 BCE as a tomb for the pharaoh Khufu. It was the largest of the three pyramids in the Giza complex and at 146.5 metres (481 ft) remained the tallest man-made artefact for over 3,800 years. Many of its 2.3 million blocks fit together with remarkable precision.

The Colossus of Rhodes

A statue of Helios, the Greek sun god, erected in 280 BCE by Chares of Lindos to celebrate victory in battle against invaders from Cyprus. Measuring 33 m (108 ft), which is about the height of the Statue of Liberty, it was destroyed in an earthquake in 226 BCE.

The Hanging Gardens of Babylon

Described as an ascending series of tiered gardens containing trees, shrubs and vines, this is the only wonder for which there is no definitive location. Legend has it that the king Nebuchadnezzar II built it for his wife, Queen Amytis of Media because she mourned for the green landscape of her homeland.

The Statue of Zeus at Olympia

Within the temple of Zeus, the sculptor Phidias created a sculpture of this greatest Greek god in about 135 BCE. He was portrayed as a giant figure seated on a wooded throne ornately embellished with ebony, ivory, gold and jewels. It was destroyed in the 5th century AD.

The Temple of Artemis

A temple at Ephesus, now in Turkey, believed to have been built in honour of the goddess Artemis in the 7th century BCE. It was destroyed and rebuilt several times (in 356 BCE by arson) before its final destruction in AD 401.

The Lighthouse (Pharos) at Alexandria

Standing at around 100 m (328 ft) the lighthouse contained a large curved mirror that projected the light of a huge fire as a beam which at night could be seen by ships up to 100 miles (161 km) away. Among the tallest buildings in the world for many centuries it was ruined by three earthquakes between AD 956 and 1323. In 1480 the last of its stones were used to build the Citadel of Qaitbay. In 1994, French archaeologists discovered some remains of the lighthouse on the seafloor, which will become part of an underwater museum.

TWO ADDITIONS In early Christian lists, Noah's Ark and the Hagia Sophia in Constantinople were added to the original seven.

The Mausoleum at Halicarnassus

Bodrum in Turkey is the modern equivalent of Halicarnassus, site of the tomb built between 353 and 350 BCE to house the mortal remains of Mausolus, a satrap in the Persian Empire, and his sister-wife Artemisia II of Caria. It measured some 45 m (148 ft) high and its four sides were adorned with reliefs, each created by one of four Greek sculptors – Leochares, Bryaxis, Scopas of Paros and Timotheus. From the 12th to the 15th centuries it was damaged by successive earthquakes before being lost for good.

MODERN WONDERS

Many different lists have been compiled of seven wonders of the modern world. A typical example comprises:
• The catacombs of Kom el Shoqafa
• The Colosseum in Rome
• The Great Wall of China
• Hagia Sophia
• The Leaning Tower of Pisa
• The Porcelain Tower of Nanjing
• Stonehenge

Other popular candidates include Petra, Machu Picchu, Christ the Redeemer in Rio, and the Taj Mahal.

The Leaning Tower of Pisa

PUZZLES TO SOLVE

THE NUMBER SEVEN HAS BEEN FEATURED IN PUZZLES THROUGHOUT THE CENTURIES AND THREE OF THEM FAMOUSLY INVOLVE THIS NUMBER. Written in around 1550 BCE, the Rhind Papyrus, which was bought in Luxor in the 1850s by the Scottish lawyer Alexander Rhind, contains 84 puzzles relating to life in ancient Egypt. Among the most famous is number 79 which runs: 'In seven houses there are seven cats. Each cat catches seven mice. If each mouse were to eat seven ears of corn and each ear of corn, if sown, were to produce seven gallons of grain, how many things are mentioned in total?

By multiplying up the steps of the puzzle the solution emerges thus:

Houses	7
Cats	49
Mice	343
Corn	2,401
Grain	16,807
Total	19,607

This very same riddle was known and quoted by Fibonacci and is almost certainly the origin of the one first printed in English in 1825:

As I was going to St Ives,
I met a man with seven wives,
Each wife had seven sacks,
Each sack had seven cats,
Each cat had seven kits:
Kits, cats, sacks, and wives,
How many were there going to St Ives?

Problem bridges

In the 18th century the East Prussian city of Königsberg (now Kaliningrad in Russia) had seven bridges. The puzzle that absorbed the people of the day was to work out whether it was possible to complete a tour of the city crossing each of the bridges only once and ending at the starting point. It was the Swiss mathematician Leonhard Euler who in 1736 proved that such a route was impossible.

Euler's proof can be represented diagrammatically by first drawing a representation of the bridges themselves and then altering it so that each bridge is represented by a line, and each area of land by a dot. If you then try to trace the lines without taking the pencil from the paper the impossibility becomes obvious. Not only did Euler solve the problem but his solution became the basis of the discipline of topology and of the maths of modern issues such as traffic flow.

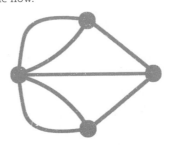

Euler's bridge solution

– HARMONY AND BALANCE

In ancient Egypt the number eight, known as the Ogdoad, was revered because it represented eight key deities. Thus it was the custom, during sacred processions on the Nile, for eight people to be present in each boat. Also significant could have been the belief that, following the Flood, only eight souls were saved from Noah's Ark – Noah and his wife, their three sons Shem, Ham and Japheth and their wives.

To the Pythagoreans eight was the number that epitomized the cycles of the earth and the regular inspiration and expiration of 'the Great Breath' that controlled them. It was also the 'full chord' or eight notes that composed a human being (see Odds and evens).

Chinese Fortune

To the Chinese, eight is associated with great fortune, not least because it sounds very similar to the word for 'prosper'. And it is no coincidence that the opening ceremony of the Beijing Olympics was timed to begin at 8 seconds and 8 minutes past 8pm on 8/8/08. The eighth day of the Chinese New Year is deemed to be the moment for the annual gathering of the gods in heaven (see Lucky – and unlucky – numbers).

Reckoning with eight

Mathematically, eight was highly regarded for being the highest even number below ten. It is the cube of two and in any number divisible by eight the last three digits are also divisible by eight. Historically there are a variety of examples of base-eight systems. Residents of California and Mexico who speak the Yuki and Pamean languages, use base eight because they count using the spaces between their fingers, not the digits themselves. In 1716 the Swedish mathematician Emanual Swedenborg was asked by his monarch, Charles XII, to devise a number system based on 64. In response Swedenborg, thinking 64 too difficult, suggested base eight instead, denoting the numbers 1 to 7 with the consonants l, s, n, m, t, f and v, and zero with the vowel o. As a result, 8 was lo, 24 no and 64 loo.

Weights and measurements

In England, 1745 saw the proposal by Hugh Jones for an octal system of calculating weights, measures and coins because it was easily divisible by two and four, although why he rejected the even more versatile imperial system based on 12 is hard to fathom. By 1801, following the introduction of the metric system in France, James Anderson suggested a base eight system which he named octal. Half a century later, Alfred B. Taylor gave numbers of his proposed base eight system new names – *un, du, the, fo, pa, se, ki* and *unty* leading to *unty-un* for 9, *unty-du* for 10 and so on. It was not until the 20th century that octal came into use in computer systems in which a byte is made up of eight bits. These have now been largely superseded by binary.

NUMBER EIGHT IN ACTION

A figure of eight is a move in skating or dance in which the number is traced out. Because such an action can theoretically carry on endlessly, the sign for infinity ∞ is an eight on its side.

A rowing eight consists of nine participants – eight oarsmen or women, plus a cox. At Oxford University Eights Week rowing competitions are part of the end of academic year celebrations in late May.

A piece of eight was the Spanish dollar, being made up of eight reales, and was used as currency in Spain until 1864. 'Pieces of eight' were the coins hidden by Long John Silver in Robert Louis Stevenson's *Treasure Island* and the clue squawked by the parrot he carried on his shoulder.

Originally, Santa Claus had eight reindeer – Dasher, Dancer, Prancer, Vixen, Comet, Cupid, Donner and Blitzen. The number increased by one when they were joined by Rudolf.

In the imperial system of measurements there are eight pints in a gallon (see By volume).

An awkward position is to be behind the eight-ball (see Snooker and other cue games).

In ancient Babylon eight gates surrounded the city, the most significant being the Gate of Ishtar named for the goddess of love and Queen of earth and heaven. A model of the gate can be seen in Berlin's Pergamon Museum.

Devout Buddhists follow the Eightfold Path which they strive to incorporate into their daily lives: Right Understanding, Right Intent, Right Speech, Right Action, Right Livelihood, Right Effort, Right Mindfulness and Right Concentration. They are represented in the eight-spoked wheel or Dharmacakra.

Austria has borders with eight other countries – Germany, Czech Republic, Slovakia, Hungary, Slovenia, Italy, Switzerland and Liechtenstein.

In an octave there are eight notes (see A musical miscellany) – and an octopus has eight arms (see The living world).

9 – A NUMBER UNBOUNDED

THRICE TO THINE AND THRICE TO MINE,
AND THRICE AGAIN MAKE UP NINE.
WITCHES' CHANT IN SHAKESPEARE'S
MACBETH.

Nine was particularly special to the Greeks because it is a trinity of trinities – 3 + 3 + 3 – and therefore a mystical number. Also known as the Ennead (which to the Egyptians comprised a group of nine deities) it was regarded as unbounded because however it is multiplied by itself, or any other single figure, the two numbers composing the product always add up to 9, as in 5 × 9 = 45, 9 × 7 = 63 and 9 × 9 = 81. Because, in this way, it unites all the numbers from 1 to 8, and because nine months is the human gestation period, it was called Concord, a name implying perfection.

A number in myth and legend

Nine recurs in the mythology of many cultures. To the Greeks, the daughters of Zeus were the nine muses who became identified with memory and with the arts and sciences, while the goddess Niobe became the personification of sorrow when her slain offspring lay in their own blood for nine days before they were buried. And the infamous

Nine peas in a pod

river Styx was believed to surround the underworld in nine circles. In Norse legend nine worlds are given life by the energy of the mystic world tree known as Yggdrasil; Hel was the goddess of the ninth of these, the abode of the dead. Every ninth night, it was believed, the god Odin's magic ring, released eight golden drops until nine golden rings were formed. When he finally sacrificed himself Odin hung on Yggdrasil for nine nights.

The theme of nine was taken up by the poet John Milton in his epic *Paradise Lost*, saying that the gates of hell were 'thrice three-fold', three being brass, three iron and three of adamantine rock. Referring to his expulsion from Mount Olympus, home of Zeus, father of the gods, Milton says that Vulcan, the god of fire, took nine days to fall to the island of Lemnos, and that the fallen angels took nine days to land after they were dispelled from heaven. In his 'Arcades' Milton includes mention of the nine spheres of which the Ptoleomeans believed the heavens to be composed.

A fortunate number

For a cat, the ability to have nine lives is undoubtedly a lucky number, as it was traditionally for unmarried young woman who found nine peas in a pod. These she would place above the door believing that the next man to enter the room would be her intended husband. To cure illness, one ancient method was to hang around a victim's neck for nine days, an abracadabra, a magical word written on parchment, which, after use, was thrown into a river to complete its healing effects. Even more direct was the practice of putting a piece of black wool knotted in nine places on a sprained ankle to effect a speedy recovery.

Like eight, nine is a significantly lucky number in Chinese culture, and when voiced it sounds very similar to the word for everlasting. It is a common custom for men to give their lovers 9 – or even 999 – roses to express his adoration. As a marriage blessing a bridegroom will still give a Red Packet containing 9,999 or 99,999 yen to his bride's family ahead of the ceremony. Even Beijing's Forbidden City is imbued with the number, having 9,999 rooms. On each gate are 81 doornails arranged in nine rows and nine columns. Virtually every staircase has nine, or a multiple of nine, treads. And the Chinese dragon, symbol of power and magic, exists in nine forms, each with nine special attributes and nine offspring.

Or maybe not
On the down side, nine is unlucky in Japan because it sounds like the word for pain. Also, seeing nine magpies together is believed to bode ill fortune and one should never give parsley as a gift because it is believed to go nine times to the Devil before its seeds (eventually) germinate. The nine of diamonds in a regular pack of playing cards is known as the 'Curse of Scotland'. This may relate to the nine lozenges that appear on the arms of the Earl of Stair, a man abhorred for his part in initiating the Glencoe massacre of 13 February 1692.

ANGELIC ORDERS

Angels are classified into nine different orders, which exist in three circles of three:

1. Seraphim, Cherubim and Thrones.

2. Dominions, Virtues and Powers.

3. Principalities, Archangels and Angels.

Chinese dragon

THE MANY MEANINGS OF NINE

A nine days' wonder is something that lasts fleetingly.

To be on cloud nine is to be in a state of perfect happiness.

Lady Jane Grey is known as the 'Nine Days' Queen – she ruled England from 10–19 July 1553 before being succeeded by Mary I, known as 'Bloody Mary'.

A cat o' nine tails is a whip with nine sections or lashes long used for beating offenders and not officially outlawed in Britain until 1944.

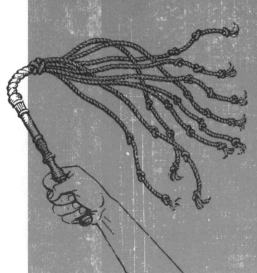

Nine men's morris is an ancient board game probably dating to Roman times, played with stones or marbles. Country folk would play it simply by fashioning lines and dips in turf or mud.

A job that is nine-to-five complies with the basic working day. It is also the title of a 1980 hit song by Dolly Parton for the film of the same name (see Counting in song).

Our solar system has nine planets Mercury, Venus, Earth, Mars, Jupiter, Saturn, Uranus, Neptune and Pluto, which was reclassified as a minor planet in 2006.

The European Union uses the refrain from Beethoven's Ninth Symphony as its anthem.

To be dressed to the nines is to be dressed to impress.

Possession, it is said, is nine-tenths of the law.

THE NINE MUSES

ORIGINALLY THREE IN NUMBER, THE NINE MUSES PRESIDED OVER POETRY AND MUSIC AND ACTED AS INSPIRATION TO WOULD-BE ARTISTS. COUNTLESS WORKS OF ART HAVE BEEN DEDICATED OVER THE CENTURIES TO THESE BEAUTIFUL WOMEN.

When the god Zeus seduced the maiden Mnemosyne he slept with her for nine consecutive nights. The result of their encounter, so the story goes, was the Nine Muses who, when they grew up, exhibited their proficiency in the arts which they were taught by Apollo. In Greek myth the Muses held poetry and musical contests with humans or semi-divine creatures – and always won. Their tactics were not always fair. In one instance they blinded the competitor Thamyris and broke his lyre.

Calliope: The 'head' Muse and protector of epic or heroic poetry. She accompanied kings and princes in order to impose justice and serenity. Homer is said to have asked her for inspiration whilst writing the *Iliad* and *Odyssey*.

Clio: Muse of history and the lyre. '*Kleos*' the Greek word for history is named after her.

Euterpe: Protector of tragedy, flute playing and lyric poetry who also played other instruments.

Thalia: The protector of comedy and idyll. Also associated with geometry, architectural science and agriculture, she was the protector of symposia.

Melpomene: The protector of tragedy and rhetoric speech. She was usually depicted holding a tragedy mask and usually bearing a bat.

Terpsichore: The Muse of dance, especially choral dance, and of the harp and education.

Erato: Protector of love and love poetry, also of hymns, lyre playing and even pantomime; also the Muse of weddings.

Polymnia: The protector of the divine hymns, mime and religious dance. She played the lyre and is also associated with geometry and grammar.

Urania: Muse of celestial objects and stars, and also celestial poetry, always depicted bearing stars, a celestial sphere and a bow compass.

Calliope   Clio   Erato

Euterpe   Melpomene   Polymnia

Terpsichore   Thalia   Urania

10 – ON OUR FINGERS AND TOES

Of all the numbers they knew and recognized, the Pythagoreans regarded ten, the Decade, as the most sacred because it brings every digit back to unity. Ten was highly significant to the practice of numerology and *kalkuli*, the pebbles they used to form the perfect triangle or tetraktys (see 4 – Truth and justice) is the source of the word 'calculate'. Ten out of ten is the maximum mark that can be scored in an examination or competition.

Counting and measuring

In practical terms, ten is a perfect base for counting simply because of the way that our hands and feet have evolved and was, of course, the basis of the decimal system of expressing numbers and the metric system of measurement. We also measure time in decades and acknowledge mathematically that to increase a figure by one order of magnitude is to multiply it by ten. The word decimate, which we now use to refer to any significant destruction, originally meant, in Roman times, the reduction of anything by one tenth. The execution of 1 in 10 soldiers in a cohort was a common retribution for mutiny or cowardice, while the lives of a tenth of the fit and able adult men were sacrificed as the price for crime or dissent within a community such as a village.

Ten is a critical number in the measurement of earthquakes on the Richter Scale named for the seismologist Charles Francis Richter who, with his Cal Tech partner Beno Gutenberg, developed their system in the 1930s. On this scale an earthquake of magnitude 6, for example, is 10 times more powerful in terms of the energy released, than one of magnitude 5. To date an earthquake measuring 10 points on the scale has never been recorded; intense destruction occurs at 6 and up (see Our planet earth).

Laws for living

It is from the Judeo-Christian tradition that we get the Ten Commandments (the Decalogue), which were engraved on a pair of stone tablets and delivered to Moses on Mount Sinai, and which over the centuries have been incorporated into Islamic belief and, in part at least, into legal systems around the world. They read:

1. I am the Lord thy God … thou shalt have no other gods before me.
2. Thou shalt not make unto thee any graven image.

Moses

3. Thou shalt not take the name of the Lord thy God in vain.
4. Remember the Sabbath day, to keep it holy.
5. Honour thy father and thy mother.
6. Thou shalt not kill.
7. Thou shalt not commit adultery.
8. Thou shalt not steal.
9. Thou shalt not bear false witness against thy neighbour.
10. Thou shalt not covet.

In agrarian societies a tithe was the income legally expected by a landowner from his tenants and comprised one tenth of the harvest.

THE POWER OF TEN

A 'tenner' is the colloquial expression for a ten-pound note or ten-dollar bill.

In his journey, following the fall of Troy and described in the *Illiad*, Odysseus roamed abroad for ten years.

The Council of Ten, instituted in 1310 and originally comprising ten members, ruled Venice as a secret cabal for over 480 years.

In Florence in 1348, during the Black Death, seven women and three men told a tale each day – or so the novelist Boccaccio imagined. His tales, famously known as *The Decameron*, and encompassing the erotic, the witty and the tragic, were probably completed around 1353.

In athletics a decathlon consists of 10 events: 100 metres, long jump, shot put, high jump, 400 metres, 110 metres hurdles, discus, pole vault, javelin and 1,500 metres, usually performed in this order.

Ten-cent Jimmy is the nickname for US President James Buchanan (1857–61) who based his government on low wages (10 cents a day) and low tariffs.

The Upper Ten is a term for the aristocracy and shorthand for the upper ten thousand. It was coined by the Boston publisher and newspaperman Nathaniel P. Willis in the mid 19th century to describe the cream of New York society.

Ten-pin bowling makes uses of ten targets – the pins – arranged in a shallow triangle. Ten frames are played in each game.

The British Prime Minister resides at Number 10 Downing Street.

11 – THE FINAL HOUR

It is at the eleventh hour that we get our last chance to rescue a situation. The expression comes from the Bible because, in the parable of the labourers in the vineyard, those who started work at 'about the eleventh hour' were paid the same as those who had worked all day. The message is that it is never too late to seek salvation. Poignantly, we still celebrate the ending of World War I in November 1918 at the 11th hour of the 11th day of the 11th month and remember the victims of the destruction of New York's Twin Towers on 9/11; the first plane to hit the North Tower of the World Trade Center was Flight 11.

To the ancients, 11 was a number of conflict and rebellion but also, because it added one to the complete cycle represented by ten, a symbol of extravagance and exaggeration. In Babylonian mythology the sea goddess Tiamat is believed to have created 11 monsters as a revenge following the death her husband Apsû. In European legend, St Ursula, a British princess, supposedly led 11 virgins on a pilgrimage to Rome in the 9th century, but when they reached Cologne, all were massacred by Huns. Over time the tale became so exaggerated that the number of virgins was increased to 11,000. Nevertheless, Christopher Columbus named the Virgin Islands after St Ursula.

Eleven days were a critical time span in 1752 when England finally followed countries of mainland Europe and changed from the Julian to the Gregorian calendar. 'Give us back our eleven days' was the cry from people who believed that they had been cheated of wages as well as the days dropped after 2 September.

ELEVEN IN CONTEXT

In popular culture the 11th commandment is said to be 'Thou shalt not be found out'.

Apollo 11 was the first manned spacecraft to reach the moon on 16 July 1969.

Elevenses are the perfect way of staving off midmorning hunger pangs.

An 11-sided shape is known as a henedecagon – and can be seen in the Indian two rupee coin.

The 'Eleventh Night' is celebrated in Northern Ireland on 11 July in commemoration of the Battle of the Boyne fought in 1690.

Eleven years of 'no fun' were those when England was ruled by the Puritan Oliver Cromwell and his son, lasting from 1649 until the restoration of Charles II as monarch in 1660.

AND THE MATHS

Eleven is the smallest two-digit prime number, being followed by 13, which makes it a twin prime (see The appeal of primes).

12 – A NUMBER IN TIME

ON THE 12TH DAY OF CHRISTMAS MY
TRUE LOVE SENT TO ME, 12 DRUMMERS
DRUMMING, 11 PIPERS PIPING ...
AND A PARTRIDGE IN A PEAR TREE.
TRADITIONAL CAROL.

It is easy to relate to the number 12, not least because there are 12 months in the year, 12 hours in the day – and the same number at night – and 12 signs in the zodiac. In imperial measurements there are 12 inches in a foot and before decimalization Britons bought and sold in shillings composed of 12 pence. And, as in the carol quoted above, there are 12 days of Christmas, ending at the eve of Epiphany, January 5th. Twelve is also a dozen, which comes from the Latin *duodecim*.

Twelve is the foundation of the duodecimal system and a most convenient number that can be divided into thirds, quarters and sixths as well as in half. This makes it easy to divide the year into four seasons and the zodiac into four groups of signs ruled by earth, air, fire and water. The Romans made good use of 12, incorporating it into the standards for measuring the size of the earth. One 12th of a whole was designated as the *unica* (the origin of ounce), which could be expressed as 24 scruples. The calculus, the smallest unit was $\frac{1}{8}$ scruples. Mathematically, 12 is the smallest of numbers known as abundant because its factors (1, 2, 3, 4, and 6) add up to 16, a number larger than itself.

The number of justice and religion

Twelve 'good men and true' is an old way of describing a jury. Certainly the so-called Wantage Code of 997 devised by King Etheldred the Unready required the 'twelve eldest *thegns*' of every district to decide on matters of innocence and guilt, but the Greeks also used a similar system. The jury system was used extensively by Henry II in the 12th century to help resolve issues relating to land and property.

Whilst 12 is a common number for jurors, in Scotland 15 is the number required for a criminal trial, while in England and Wales county courts use juries of only eight members. Since the 13th century women had been allowed on juries with the specific purpose of determining whether women on trial were pregnant (and therefore temporarily spared the fate of execution) but not until 1919 were women allowed to serve routinely in Britain. And only in 1973 did all 50 states of America admit women to juries on terms equal to those of their male counterparts.

The Hebrew Bible tells us that the 12 sons of Jacob – Ruben, Simeon, Levi, Judah, Dan, Naphtali, Gad, Asher, Issachar, Zebulun, Josef and Benjamin – were the founders of the 12 tribes of Israel. In the New Testament's Book of Revelation the author's vision of New

Jerusalem is of 12,000 members of each tribe being afforded salvation on the last day, and of the tribe names being inscribed on each of 12 gates, three each on north, south, east and west. Also significant is that Jesus took 12 disciples to aid him in his mission.

The flag of the European Union, officially adopted on 8 December 1955, bears a circle of 12 yellow stars and relates to the verse in Revelation that runs: 'And a great portent appeared in heaven, a woman clothed with the sun, with the moon under her feet, and on her head a crown of twelve stars.' The number

BY TWELVE

The 'glorious twelfth', 12 August, is the date on which grouse shooting officially begins each year in Britain.

Shakespeare named his play *Twelfth Night* because he intended it to be performed on the final day of the Christmas season.

The Chinese zodiac denotes 12 animals of which the most renowned is the dragon.

It is said that to ensure good luck for the coming year you should eat one grape on each of the 12 chimes of midnight on New Year's Eve.

In carrying out his renowned penance, Hercules completed 12 extraordinary labours.

The Greek pantheon comprises 12 Olympians: Zeus, Hera, Poseidon, Demeter, Athena, Apollo, Artemis, Ares, Aphrodite, Hephaestos, Hermes and Dionysus (or Hestia). They reside atop Mount Olympus.

A solid with 12 faces is known as a dodecahedron. A flat shape (polygon) with 12 sides is a dodecagon.

A baker's dozen is usually 13 but can be 14 or 15. It was a man's insurance against providing less than the required weight of bread in his loaves.

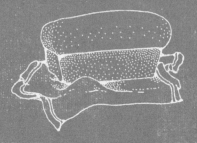

To talk nineteen to the dozen is to babble on without pause.

A Devil's dozen is 13. As is a long dozen.

was chosen for its significance to every country in the group. As the official description states: 'Their number shall be invariably set to twelve, the symbol of completeness and perfection.'

Effecting a cure
In the treatment of addictions and other behavioural problems the 12-step program originally proposed by the American William Griffith (Bill) Wilson in 1939 continues to be effective. Wilson, himself an alcoholic, was the founder of Alcoholics Anonymous. In essence, these involve admitting that one cannot control one's condition; recognizing a higher power that can confer strength; examining past errors with the help of a sponsor; making amends for these errors; learning to live a new life; and helping others suffering similar problems.

THE TWELVE LABOURS OF HERCULES

HE HAD BEEN DRIVEN MAD BY THE GODDESS HERA, SISTER AND CONSORT OF ZEUS AND, AS A RESULT COMMITTED A SERIES OF MURDERS. SO IT WAS THAT THE GREEK HERO HERCULES (HERACLES) COMMITTED HIMSELF TO EXILE.
After travelling to Delphi to consult the god Apollo, Hercules was commanded to serve king Eurystheus of Mycenae (who had been enthroned by the hated Hera) for 12 years with the promise that, once his tasks were completed, he would become immortal and take his place among the gods. Reluctantly Hercules set out on his dozen labours.

Task One: Bring the hide of the Nemean Lion
The pelt of the lion proved impossible to pierce with an arrow shot from a bow, so Hercules stunned it with an olive-wood club. The lion retreated to a cave but the hero wrestled it into submission and strangled it, then removed the skin, wrapped it around himself, and returned with the carcass over his shoulder. Eurystheus was terrified and asked that in future Hercules' trophies be left outside the city gates. He himself hid in a huge bronze jar buried under the ground.

Task Two: Kill the Hydra of Lerna
The monstrous marsh-dwelling Hydra, with a dog-like body and many serpentine heads (probably seven) devoured people and animals. Even her foul breath was deadly. Hercules attacked her with a sword and shot flaming arrows at her, but as one head was destroyed another grew in its place. So Hercules ordered his helpmate Iolaus,

Task Three: Capture alive the Cerynthian Hind

(his nephew), to sear each wound with
burning branches. His remaining arrows,
dipped in Hydra's blood, became deadly.
However Eurystheus refused to accept
the labour as completed since Hercules
had been helped.

Task Three: Capture alive the Cerynthian Hind

It took Hercules almost a year to chase
and catch this beautiful beast with
golden antlers and brass hooves, loved
by the goddess Artemis. On his way back
with the creature, Hercules encountered
Artemis who chastised him for his insult
to her, but excused him and sent him on
his way once the blame had been passed
instead to Eurystheus.

Task Four: Capture the Erymanthian Boar

Hercules cunningly lured the boar,
which was ravaging the local population,
out of hiding and into the forest where
he managed to push it into a snow-filled
ravine. He then wrapped it in chains.
Travelling back to the king he was set
upon by centaurs who hurled tree
trunks and rocks at him. However the
hero successfully killed his attackers
and completed his task.

Task Five: Clean the Augeian Stables

A single day was all Hercules was
given for his task for which the king
Augeias agreed to give him one tenth
of the cows. First Hercules tore down
a wall then diverted the waters of two
great rivers to facilitate the cleansing.

Deeming it a 'job for hire' Eurystheus refused to accept this accomplishment.

Task Six: Dispel the Stymphalian Birds

Vast congregations of these birds with bronze beaks, claws and wings, fed on animals, men and women. Luckily for Hercules he was given some bronze castanets by the goddess Athena and created such a din that the birds took off in one huge flock and disappeared. Many were killed with Hercules' poison arrows; others flew far off and failed to return.

Task Seven: Capture the Cretan Bull

On Crete, the Bull believed to be the Minotaur's father ravaged crops and orchards. Not only did Hercules

capture the creature but succeeded in bringing it back across the sea to present it to Eurystheus. The Bull was then set free only to be killed, much later, by Theseus.

Task Eight: Capture the Mares of Diomedes

Hercules had to capture four of these savage mares, fed with the flesh of innocent strangers. When he managed to steal the horses and drive them into the sea Diomedes – and many of his subjects – pursued him but Hercules first killed the subjects then murdered the king and fed him to his own mares. Finally, Hercules harnessed the horses to Diomedes' chariot and drove them back to Eurystheus.

Task Eight: Capture the Mares of Diomedes

Hercules and the Oxen of Geryones

Task Nine: Obtain the Belt of Hippolyte

Hippolyte, queen of the Amazons, had been given her fabulous belt by Ares, the god of war. Initially, Hippolyte agreed to give Hercules the belt, but to obtain it he eventually had to kill her after he was attacked by the Amazons who believed, thanks to a rumour spread by Hera, that he was planning to abduct their queen.

Task Ten: Fetch the Cattle of Geryon

Spain was Hercules' next destination, to find cattle owned by a giant with three upper bodies and guarded by a two-headed dog Orthus and another giant, Eurytion. He used a poison arrow to pierce all three of Geryon's bodies and killed Orthus and Eurytion with a club. When he finally reached Eurystheus, having been helped out by Zeus, just one ox remained, which was sacrificed to Hera.

Task Eleven: Obtain the Three Golden Apples of Hesperides

The fabulous fruit-bearing tree was tended by nymphs and defended by Ladon, a 100-headed dragon. Above it stood the giant Atlas. Having killed Ladon, Hercules struck a bargain with Atlas who fetched the apples while Hercules held up the sky in his stead. Hercules finally secured the fruit and gave them to the king.

Task Twelve: Capture Cerberus

Hercules entered the blackness of Hades to encounter Cerberus, the hideous three-headed guard dog of the underworld. There the ruler of the underworld gave permission for the capture of Cerberus as long as Hercules used his bare hands. The successful hero returned to earth and, having presented the hound to Eurythsenes, returned it to the underworld.

His penance completed, Hercules carried out many more daring and dangerous feats. After his death his body was cremated and his soul ascended to Olympus where he made peace with Hera and married Hebe.

13 – AND OTHER TEENS

I AM SIXTEEN GOING ON SEVENTEEN/I
KNOW THAT I'M NAIVE …. SONG LYRICS
FROM THE SOUND OF MUSIC (1965)

Thirteen, renowned for its association with ill fortune (see Lucky – and unlucky – numbers)) does have positive connotations for Italians who regard it as lucky. For them to 'hit the jackpot' is to 'do 13' or *'fare tredici'*. It is also lucky for Colgate University, New York, having been founded in 1819 by 13 men with 13 dollars, 13 prayers and 13 articles. In the standard pack or deck of cards, which may bring good luck or ill, there are four suits of 13 cards each.

Thirteen is key to the inaugural flag of the USA where 13 five-pointed stars, set from 1792 in a circle at the top left, and its 13 stripes, represented the original 13 colonies. In American folk history the creation of the flag is credited to needlewoman Elizabeth Griscom 'Betsy' Ross, and although this is now disputed she certainly made flags for the Pennsylvania Navy during the American Revolution. The design has been changed many times – the current design with its 50 stars is number 27.

John 'Sixteen String' Rann was a notorious 18th-century highwayman named from the 16 coloured strings that he wore attached to his breeches. He is said to have danced a jig before being hanged at Tyburn on 30 November 1774.

A miscellany of meanings

Fourteen is the number of days in a fortnight and the number of lines in a sonnet. Beethoven's famous 'Moonlight Sonata' is designated No.14. Historically, the Fourteen Points were the 14 conditions laid down by US President Woodrow Wilson which he believed necessary to end World War I. There are 15 days in each of the 24 cycles of the Chinese calendar, and in British history The Fifteen is the name of the 1715 Jacobite rebellion in which the Old Pretender James Edward Stewart unsuccessfully attempted to gain the throne.

Sixteen is the easily divisible number used for weighing light objects in several cultures, as in the 16 ounces in the British pound. Chinese Taoists were once adept at using their thumbs to count the tips and joints of the fingers, making 16 on each hand. In Italy 17, written XVII in Roman numerals, is deemed unlucky because when rearranged it reads VIXI, meaning 'I have lived'. Mathematically, 17 is the only prime number which is the sum of four consecutive primes (2,3,5,7). Any other four consecutive primes added together always produce an even number.

In ancient Rome the number 18 symbolized a blood relative while for the

Chinese, 18 is a lucky number because it sounds very similar to 'definitely get rich'. The Hindu scripture the Bhagavad Gita is divided in to 18 chapters. The 'ka-ete of 19' or 'Directive Nineteen' is a powerful key in author Stephen King's multivolume epic *The Dark Tower* and the popular game of Go is played on a 19 × 19 grid.

GROWING UP – WHAT TEENAGERS CAN AND CAN'T DO

13 – Traditional age for Jewish boys to become (and undergo the ceremony of) a Bar Mitzvah, a full member of the faith.

14 – Most common age of criminal responsibility in Europe (but is a mere 10 in England and Wales).

15 – Legal to undertake work in the UK but for restricted hours.

16 – Minimum age for obtaining an adult passport in the USA, UK and Australia. Age of sexual consent in the UK, and in Scotland the minimal age for marriage without parental consent and voting in local elections and referendum.

17 – In the UK and many other countries, the minimum age for a driving licence.

18 – Voting age for general elections in most countries.

19 – Minimum age for drinking and buying alcohol in Canada except in provinces Alberta, Manitoba, and Quebec.

0 – THE STORY OF ZERO

FROM ZERO TO HERO –/IN NO TIME FLAT/ZERO TO HERO–/JUST LIKE THAT. **FROM DISNEY'S** *HERCULES*, **1997.**

Although not technically a number, zero gets its name from the Arabic word *sifr*, which is the derivation of the English word cipher, the symbol that plays such a large part in the way that we express and interpret numbers. Nought or naught, nil and, in a number context 'oh', are other ways of signifying zero which in tennis is simply 'love'.

Before the invention of zero the Babylonians used wedge marks to show that there was unoccupied space between numbers so as to distinguish, for example, 606 from 66, and while some ancient Greek astronomers inserted a letter O in their workings they had no real concept of 'nothingness'.

It was in India, in the 2nd century BCE, that the use of zero truly originated as a means of indicating an empty place in a number. A key mathematician in the eventual widespread adoption

ALSO ZERO Across the world the Maya of Central America invented zero quite independently in the 4th century. When written, it took the shape of a snail shell and was used to fill the gaps in their 'long count' system which was, to all intents and purposes, base 20.

of zero was Brahmagupta (born in AD 598) whose work entitled *Brahmasphutasiddhanta* contained many mathematical findings written in verse form. Centuries later, in 976 a definitive statement was made by Muhammed ibn Ahmad al-Khwarizmi that if, in a calculation, no number appears in the place of tens then a little circle should be employed to 'keep the rows'.

In Europe, the key character in the acceptance of zero was the Italian mathematician Fibonacci (see the brilliant number sequence), who first described it in around 1200. However it took many more years for Europeans to become comfortable and familiar with the Arabic system of numerals which included zero. It was only with the development and spread of printing that it became part of everyday life.

Zero in life

In our everyday lives, zero is key to the digital language used to programme our computers and we know that zero degrees Centigrade is the freezing point of water. When we talk of zero hour we are in fact using a term that originated during World War I for the timing of

LOWEST POSSIBLE Absolute zero, the lowest temperature possible, has been calculated to be -373.15° degrees Centigrade or -460° degrees Fahrenheit.

a military operation. If overdue, it was said to be occurring at, say, zero + 4.

The first 10 years of the 21st century are dubbed the 'noughties', and there was much trepidation (and preparatory work) amongst businesses worldwide when the date changed from 1999 to 2000 that computer systems would crash with devastating effects. In the event, no such disaster occurred.

LUCKY – AND UNLUCKY – NUMBERS

ASK ANYONE 'WHAT IS YOUR LUCKY NUMBER?' AND THERE IS A GOOD CHANCE THAT THEY WILL ANSWER 'SEVEN'. HOWEVER THERE IS FAR FROM TOTAL CONSISTENCY, AND THE NUMBERS ASSOCIATED WITH GOOD FORTUNE AND BAD DIFFER BETWEEN CULTURES.

The number seven is special because it is the number of the days of the week, the ages of man and the gifts of the Holy Spirit. The pinnacle of ecstasy or good fortune is said to lead us to seventh heaven, and the rainbow – God's signal, after the Flood, of his treaty with humankind – is composed of seven colours. But break a mirror and, it is said, you will have seven years' bad luck. In Japan, seven is the number of the Gods of Fortune whose

IN THREES

To be third time lucky is said by some to have originated from the fate of a convicted murderer John 'Babbacombe' Lee who survived three attempts at hanging for his crime on the same day in February 1885, although there is evidence for the phrase being used in Scotland in 1868. The superstition lives on that three candles burning in a room harbingers bad luck as is hearing an owl hoot three times. And of course few girls want to be 'three times a bridesmaid, never a bride'.

faces are customarily carved as netsuke and worn on a sash around the waist to give protection from harm. These are believed to have power over wealth, longevity and the abundance of food from both land and sea and to bring beauty and happiness.

It is eight that is particularly lucky in China and Japan because the word for the number sounds very similar to 'prosper'. Here, countries' vendors habitually put the number eight into a price, such as $85.88 to make it more attractive to prospective buyers. In 2003 a telephone number consisting entirely of eights was sold in China for 2.33 million yen. And it is no accident that the Olympic Games of 2008 were scheduled to begin on the 8th day of the 8th month (August).

The number three is also commonly associated with fortune. The Pythagoreans revered it as the number of the great virtues needed for married bliss, namely justice, fortitude and prudence. Just as we give three cheers for a fortunate event and believe that we can be third time lucky, so it's commonly held that accidents happen in runs of three then stop – for a while, at least. That three, the number of the trinity, is also an odd number may be significant, too (see 3 – The trinity of perfection).

Unlucky thirteen

When, on Good Friday, Jesus sat down to the Last Supper there were 13 people at the table. The thirteenth, Judas Iscariot, was soon to betray him, an act that culminated in Christ's crucifixion. So 13, and especially Friday the 13th, is believed to have gained its association with bad luck.

From this belief stems the superstition that 13 people should never sit at a table together or one of the party will die within the year, most probably the person who is first to rise from their chair. Similarly, one member of a ship's crew of 13 is believed to be destined for a fatal accident, 13 being known to mariners as 'the Devil's lot'. Or 13 could come from the number in a witches' coven, the 13th being the most evil. That 13 is a 'baker's dozen' may come from Boucca's dozen – Boucca being a spirit in Cornish lore.

Irrational fear of the number 13 is known as triskaidekaphobia. In many streets, houses are numbered 12A rather than 13 and the same can apply to the numbering of the floors in some skyscrapers. Or 13 may be omitted altogether. On the good side, 13

The number 13 is significant to Australian cricketers. For them 87 is the unluckiest number because it is 13 short of a century.

represents St Anthony, the patron saint whose powers are believed to be able to help you find lost things.

... and four

Superstitions about numbers exist worldwide. To those whose first language is Mandarin, Cantonese, Japanese or Korean four is unlucky because the word sounds very similar to 'death'. This belief is held so strongly that among Chinese and Japanese Americans the chances of dying from a fatal heart attack on the 4th of the month are seven per cent higher than average. As with 13 in the West, four is avoided for numbering the floors of buildings, apartments and the like.

Lucky or not?

Numbers are a sensitive issue when it comes to magpies – seeing a lone bird is bad, but two or more are lucky, as in the rhyme 'One for sorrow, two for joy, three for a girl, four for a boy...'

The number of times you sneeze may be significant to fortune. Sneeze once and someone is speaking well of you, sneeze twice and the reverse is true. Or test your luck according to the verse:

Once a wish
Twice a kiss
Three times something better.

Luckiest of all is for two people to sneeze simultaneously.

666, the Number of the Beast in the Book of Revelation is a figure to be dreaded in Christian cultures but to the Chinese is lucky because it is divisible by both two and three and means that everything goes smoothly.

PURELY SUPERSTITIOUS?

Numbers appear in all manner of other superstitions and superstitious behaviours over the centuries:

• It was once customary to take a sick child to a blacksmith of the seventh generation and lay him or her naked on the anvil to effect a cure.

• If you find a four-holed button, pick it up and keep it for luck.

• The four of clubs is the unluckiest card in the pack.

• An egg with two yolks means that a wedding is on the way.

• If a bachelor makes three notches on a five-barred gate and repeats the action for nine nights he is sure to find a sweetheart.

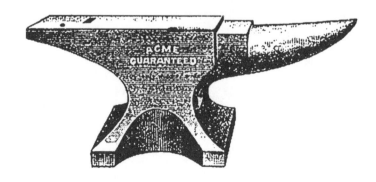

ODDS AND EVENS

WHETHER ODD NUMBERS ARE MORE POTENT THAN EVEN ONES DEPENDS ON BOTH CULTURE AND CUSTOM, BUT THE DIFFERENCE BETWEEN THEM MAY LIE DEEP IN THE HUMAN PSYCHE.

To the ancient Sumerians, odd numbers were male and even ones female, a belief endorsed by Pythagoras in the 6th century BCE, who thought that because odd numbers cannot be split exactly into two they are stronger than weaker, feminine ones, that can be so divided. He believed that, because they remain odd when added to even numbers, odd numbers were the masters of even ones.

Number psychology

It appears that odd numbers lodge in our brains more firmly than even ones because they are harder to 'digest'. This may be due, in part, to the fact that ten, the number of our fingers and toes is an even number and possibly because even numbers appear more often in the times tables we learn in school than odd numbers. In an experiment in which people were shown pairs of numbers and asked to press a button each time they saw two odd numbers (say 3 and 7) or two even numbers (say 2 and 8) it took them 20 per cent longer to 'process' the pairs of odd numbers, seemingly because they demand more effort from our brains.

It is most probably

TOOTH PAIN
To prevent toothache, Pliny advocated washing the mouth out with cold water every morning 'an odd number of times'.

the 'special effect' of odd numbers that makes Room 101 in George Orwell's *Nineteen Eighty-Four* a much scarier place than Room 100 would have been. Maria Milikowski of the University of Amsterdam showed the participants in a study all the numbers between 1 and 100 and asked them to designate each as bad or good, calm or excitable. Overwhelmingly odd numbers were seen as bad, evens as good and calming. Those ending in 1, 2 or 3 were deemed most excitable. This might explain why WD-40 has the comforting prospect of being a product that will do exactly what it promises (although the skin cream E45 is arguably equally effective in its own way). And Douglas Adams, author of *A Hitchhiker's Guide to the Galaxy* chose 42 as the answer to the ultimate question of 'life, the universe and everything' because it was an 'ordinary, smallish number' and created the anticlimax he intended.

Many people deem it unlucky to have an odd number of people seated around the table or at a funeral party, when it is said that the corpse will call for another soul to even up the numbers. Odd numbers (with the notable exception of 13) are widely considered lucky for, as the Roman poet Virgil noted in around 40 BCE: 'Odd numbers please the gods'. To the Chinese, by contrast, even numbers are generally considered lucky because for them good luck comes in pairs.

AN ODD ARRANGEMENT

Odd numbers are crucial to the Japanese art of *ikebana*, symbolic flower arranging because, according to Buddhist beliefs, asymmetry is the perfect reflection of the natural world. In the Oriental philosophy of yin and yang, the soft, feminine yin is associated with even numbers and the robust yang with odd numbers – and also good fortune.

MANY FAVOURITE NUMBERS

ASIDE FROM LUCK, OR WHETHER THEY ARE ODD OR EVEN, NUMBERS CAN CREATE AN ESPECIAL FONDNESS. THESE NUMBERS, WHICH WE FAVOUR AS PIN NUMBERS AND IN PASSWORDS FOR THE MANY TRANSACTIONS WE CONDUCT EVERY DAY, MAY RELATE TO A BIRTHDAY, A SIGNIFICANT EVENT, OR SOME SATISFACTORY MATHEMATICAL QUALITY.

For the ancient Babylonians, 60 was the most significant number, on which all their mathematics and their calendar was based. Today, seven is the most popular number for all kinds of reasons closely followed by three. Of all the numbers between one and ten, it is seven that feels most 'random' says British mathematician and writer Alex Bellos. When asked by psychologists to choose a two-digit number less than 50, both numbers being odd and excluding 11, but allowing 13, more than a third of an experimental group chose 37. Of the

possible numbers – 13, 15, 17, 19, 31, 35, 37 and 39 it was deemed 'exotic' as well as being prime.

In his researches Bellos has also discovered that while we do not particularly like numbers ending in 0 or 5, we do like those that have a pattern or have some personal significance and so are our 'friends'. Among the favoured numbers, his surveys revealed, were 6 because it was the favourite track on an album, 17 because it was the number of minutes that rice took to cook and 1,000,000,007 because it was the largest prime number the respondent could remember. The appeal of 120 was that it is divisible by 2,3,4,5,6,8 and 10.

Shopping by numbers

It is no accident that vendors favour prices such as £89, €29.99 and $7.99, whether we are buying cars, clothes or pizza. Because we respond more strongly to the first digit than the last, in our heads there is not much difference between £89 and £88 but a significant one between £89 and £90. However when researchers at MIT asked mail order shoppers to choose between the same dress priced at $34, $39 and $44 the majority chose the one at $39. And it is not necessarily the number alone. Restaurateurs have discovered that listing food on a menu as simply 10.50 rather than as £10.50 or $10.50 creates significantly more sales.

THE TAXICAB NUMBER

In 1918 when the Indian mathematical genius Srinivasa Ramanujan was seriously ill in hospital he was visited by his mentor Professor Geoffrey Hardy. Learning that Hardy had travelled by taxi, Ramanujan asked him the taxi number. Hardy replied that it was a boring 1729. Not boring at all, replied Ramanujan, explaining that it was the smallest number that could be expressed by the sum of two positive cubes in two different ways, namely 13 + 123 or 93 + 103 cubed. Today, 1,729 is sometimes called the Hardy-Ramanujan number.

THE SESAME STREET SURVEY

In 2012 the BBC ran a piece marking the death of puppeteer Jerry Nelson, inventor of *Sesame Street*'s Count von Count, whose favourite number was 34,969 or 187^2. Respondents – doubtless adult fans of the children's hit show – were invited to share their favourites, which included:

2 – the only even prime number.

17 – a small number greater than 1 that is the sum of a square and a cube.
17 = 9+8
$= 3^2 + 2^3$

26 – the only number that sits between a perfect square (25) and a perfect cube (27).

211 – not only the respondent's birthday (2 November) but because 2, 11 and 211 are all primes.

11,235,813 – representing the Fibonacci series (see the brilliant number sequence).

1,025 – the approximate number of molecules in a glass of wine.

THE SECRETS OF NUMEROLOGY

THE BELIEF THAT THERE IS A SIGNIFICANT, MYSTICAL LINK BETWEEN NUMBERS AND EVENTS IS THE ANCIENT FOUNDATION OF NUMEROLOGY, ALTHOUGH THE WORD ITSELF DID NOT FORMALLY ENTER THE ENGLISH LANGUAGE UNTIL 1907. LINKS BETWEEN NUMBERS AND LETTERS OF THE ALPHABET ARE PARTICULARLY SIGNIFICANT TO ITS CONCLUSIONS AND PREDICTIONS.

Although the ancient Egyptians attributed importance to numbers and used them to predict the future, it was the Greek mathematician Pythagoras who significantly influenced the development of numerology. Believing that numbers are the key to understanding the hidden secrets of the universe and its evolution, he called his theory the Science of Numbers, which is also known as the Doctrine of Emanations. According to Pythagoras the significant features of numbers one to ten were:

■ 1 Unity, and therefore indivisible. Also representative of the Deity.

■ 2 Diversity and, by definition, disorder. The embodiment of the tussle between good and evil.

■ 3 Perfect harmony, the union between unity and diversity. Represented in the triangle, the most profound geometrical symbol.

■ 4 Perfection, and the 'key bearer of Nature' and the first square, product of 2×2.

■ 5 Represented by the five-pointed star and associated with the Ether, the fifth element. Regarded as the prevailing number in both nature and art.

■ 6 Symbolized by two interlaced triangles, number 6 unifies matter and spirit, male and female.

■ 7 Significantly combines the principles of 3 and 4, giving it perfect qualities. In disease, the climacteric or 'high point' of an infection.

■ 8 Justice and an expression of eternal motion in the universe.

■ 9 Represents both the ocean and the horizon within which all numbers revolve.

■ 10 A return to unity and significant as the total of 1 + 2 + 3 + 4.

MUSICAL INFLUENCES

It is believed by some that it was Pythagoras' discovery that in music the octave, the fifth and the fourth can be expressed as simple ratios between the numbers 1, 2, 3 and 4 which had a profound effect on his belief that numbers are the influence guiding the universe and the world around us.

Pythagoras

According to these designations, numbers 1 to 3 represent the 'higher' or metaphysical world, those from 4 to 9 the physical aspects of the world. Odd numbers were regarded as male and even ones as female. For Pythagoreans, the number 10 was represented in a *tetraktys*, a sacred symbol of 10 dots arranged in a triangle (see 4 – truth and justice) on which they swore this oath:

I swear by him who the Tetraktys found,
Whence all our wisdom springs and which contains
Perennial Nature's fountain, cause and root.

By the Middle Ages, religion had a bearing on numerology and St Augustine of Hippo (354–430) wrote that numbers are 'the Universal language offered by the deity to humans as confirmation of the truth', but such beliefs were outlawed following the First Council of Nicaea in 325 as deviations from state church beliefs and therefore civil violations. While Sir Thomas Brown's 1658 *The Garden of Cyrus* attempted to prove the influence of the number five in art, design and nature there were few developments until the 1970s when Dr Juno Jordan published the popular work *The Romance in Your Name* based on numerological principles.

How it works

The principle behind numerology is that every letter of the alphabet corresponds to a number. The so-called 'Latin' system works in this way:

1	2	3	4	5	6	7	8	9
a	b	c	d	e	f	g	h	i
j	k	l	m	n	o	p	q	r
s	t	u	v	w	x	y	z	

To calculate your name number, say Maria Tucker, add the numbers for each letter, first of the given name, which is 24, giving 2 + 4 = 6. Then do the same for the surname, which also equals 24, giving 6 as the key number.

To find a personal birth number, say 20 September 1957 (for Maria Tucker) add each element of the date in this way: 20 + 9 + 1 + 5 + 7 = 42. Then add the 4 and the 2 to get 6. Those with this number are believed to be idealists and lovers of harmony (see chart). When, as here, a person's numbers are identical – 6 in this instance – then they are said to possess unique and special qualities.

The same system of ascribing numbers to letters can be made for the place where you live – both the town or city and the street. Thus London gives you the number 5 (perhaps the ultimate all-rounder) while New York calculates to 3 (forceful and frank).

There are variations on this pattern, significantly the Chaldean system, the oldest type of numerology, which originated in Babylon, probably in the 7th century. In this, numbers representing letters range only from 1 to 8. Number 9 is omitted because it is deemed to be holy. Equally ancient is the Kabbalah system of numerology, based on ancient Hebrew mysticism, specifically, the Hebrew alphabet and means 'knowledge that comes through the mind and soul'. In seeking to bring insight through self awareness it is based solely on a person's name.

Character influences

The way in which a person's character links with their personal number varies from system to system, but the pertinent characteristics to consider in each are shown opposite:

Tenacious, independent and reliable. Likely to be ambitious high achievers. May be intolerant, conceited and obstinate.

Balanced, cooperative and sympathetic. Adaptable and pragmatic but may lack forcefulness.

Forceful, frank and creative, also cheerful, sociable and appreciative of the arts. Can be over-confident and impatient.

Stable, loyal and tenacious. Faithful friends but inclined to dullness and conservatism.

Adventurous, courageous and vivacious. All-rounders and good communicators with a positive attitude but can be rash and irresponsible.

Idealists and lovers of harmony, likely to be healers and counsellors. Faithful and loving but soft hearted.

Wise and discerning, also skilled mediators. Strong on self-discipline, they need solitude to an extent that they may undervalue friendship.

Powerful and organized with good judgement, especially in business and wealth creation. Often tactless and domineering.

Intelligent and scholarly, understanding and humanitarian. Appreciate the arts but may be dreamy, lethargic and unambitious.

BIG NUMBERS

'I'D WALK A MILLION MILES FOR ONE OF YOUR SMILES', AS THE SONG GOES, IS A PERFECT EXAMPLE OF THE WAY EXAGGERATIONS CAN EXPRESS BIG NUMBERS. BUT HUGE NUMBERS, PROPERLY DENOTED AND USED, ARE VITAL TO THE CALCULATIONS EMPLOYED IN SCIENCE AND MATHEMATICS.

Although it seems specific, the number 40, as in the '40 days and 40 nights' of rain in the Old Testament flood is traditionally used throughout the Middle East to mean a large number. Similarly in Arabic *The Book of One Thousand and One Nights* (see Books with numbers) refers to a long period of time while 1,001, as in 1,001 *Hints and Tips* is marketing shorthand for many. The word 'umpteen' is believed to derive from 'umpty-seven', umpty being a dash in Morse code and implying a multiple of ten.

While a million, written 1,000,000 or a thousand thousands (also expressed as 10^5) is relatively easy to comprehend, as in the populations of countries, it would actually be impossible for a human to walk that number of miles in a lifetime. A billion – now universally agreed to be a thousand million or 1,000,000,000 – is harder to grasp. There are more than a billion webpages on the internet and if a person were to live to 95 they would have survived for around 3 billion

EXAGGERATING NUMBERS

Now simply called 'sprinkles' the multicoloured sugar strands used to decorate a cake or finish an ice cream were once known as 'hundreds and thousands'.

In an effort to impress, it is common to make an impossible promise of putting in 110 per cent. Or one might go beyond the call of duty by pledging to work – or love – for 8 days a week.

seconds since their birth.

Larger yet are the trillion or 1,000,000,000,000 and quadrillion or 1,000,000,000,000,000. There are around 50 trillion cells in a human body and it is said that the entire financial assets of everyone on earth amount to about a quadrillion US dollars.

As with million and the like, the names of other big numbers have Latin origin. Some examples include:

Name	Number of zeros
Quintillion	18 (1,000,000,000,000,000,000)
Sextillion	21 (1,000,000,000,000,000,000,000)
Septillion	24 (1,000,000,000,000,000,000,000,000)
Octillion	27 (1,000,000,000,000,000,000,000,000,000)
Nonillion	30 (1,000,000,000,000,000,000,000,000,000,000)
Decillion	33 (1,000,000,000,000,000,000,000,000,000,000,000)

Words such as zillion, gazillion and squillion are used as hyperbole for vast numbers. However the googol, for which the search engine Google was named, is the number 10 to the power 100 (10^{100}), written as 1 followed by 100 zeros. From this follows the googolplex, which is 1 followed by 10^{100} zeros. Numbers such as these are used to specify quantities such as the grains of sand in deserts or distances in the universe.

Sagan's number, named for the American cosmologist Carl Sagan, is an estimate of the number of stars in the universe. In 1980 Sagan himself reckoned it to be 10 sextillion, but by 2010 the number had already risen to 300 sextillion.

SMALL NUMBERS

ON THE TAPE MEASURES AND RULERS WE USE DAY TO DAY THE MILLIMETER, ONE THOUSANDTH OF A METRE, IS THE SMALLEST MEASUREMENT PROVIDED, AND IS PERFECTLY ADEQUATE FOR MOST OF THE TASKS WE NEED TO PERFORM. AS SCIENCE AND TECHNOLOGY PROGRESS, THE NEED FOR USING VERY SMALL NUMBERS INCREASES MASSIVELY.

A simple way to express the millimeter notationally is as 1×10^{-3} m. Scientists manipulating matter at the atomic level make use of the nanometer which is 1×10^{-9} or one millionth of a millimetre. Even smaller is the Ångström unit (Å), named for the Swedish physicist and astronomer Anders Ångström (1814–74), which is a tenth smaller than the nanometer or 1×10^{-10} m. The diameter of a hydrogen atom, for example is 0.5 Å. Smaller yet are the picometre (1×10^{-12} m), the femtometre (1×10^{-15} m), the attometre (1×10^{-18} m), the zeptometre (1×10^{-21} m) and the yocometre (1×10^{-24} m).

The very smallest

To date, the smallest length that it is possible to measure, is known as Planck's constant, named for the German physicist Max Planck (1858–1947) who first calculated it in 1900. The figure, which relates to the speed of light, is a staggering 1.616×10^{-35} m. Lengths smaller than this are not believed to have any physical substance – at least in the way in which we currently understand the universe.

Anders Ångström

ALSO SMALL

Some other very small numbers have significance in our universe, for example: A stationary electron weighs approximately 9.11×10^{-31} kg, while a proton weighs 1.673×10^{-27} kg. A neutron is just a little heavier at 1.675×10^{-27} kg.

THE APPEAL OF PRIMES

OF ALL THE MANY TYPES OF NUMBERS THAT CAN BE DESCRIBED, THOSE THAT HAVE LONG AROUSED GREATEST INTEREST AND AFFECTION ARE PRIMES, THE NUMBERS THAT CAN BE DIVIDED SOLELY BY ONE OR THEMSELVES.

The prize of modern prime 'addicts' are so-called Olympic Gold primes with millions of digits discovered with the help of computers. Echoing sentiments that persist today the Swiss 18th-century mathematician Leonhard Euler said: 'Mathematicians have tried in vain to discover some order in the sequence of prime numbers and we have reason to believe that it is a mystery into which the human mind will never penetrate.'

Going back to the beginning, the first few primes are well known, being 2, 3, 5, 7, 11, 13, 17, 19, 23 .... (Note that 1, though once considered prime is not included.) If a number is not prime, then it is said to be composite, and can be arrived at by multiplying together two or more prime numbers – a fact established by Euclid, the famous ancient Greek who lived around 300 BCE. Some simple examples are $4 = 2 \times 2$; $6 = 2 \times 3$; $8 = 2 \times 2 \times 2$; $9 = 3 \times 3$; $10 = 2 \times 5$; $12 = 2 \times 2 \times 3$ ....

Is it a prime?

In order to make it easier to identify primes, the Greek mathematician, poet, astronomer and musician Eratosthenes designed a 'sieve' to more easily identify those numbers that were primes and those which are composite. It looks like this:

1	**2**	**3**	4	**5**	6	**7**	8	9	10
11	12	**13**	14	15	16	**17**	18	**19**	20
21	22	**23**	24	25	26	27	28	**29**	30
31	32	33	34	35	36	**37**	38	39	40
41	42	**43**	44	45	46	**47**	48	49	50
51	52	**53**	54	55	56	57	58	**59**	60
61	62	63	64	65	66	**67**	68	69	70
71	72	**73**	74	75	76	77	78	**79**	80
81	82	**83**	84	85	86	87	88	**89**	90
91	92	93	94	95	96	**97**	98	99	100

Ertosthenes' sieve

As you can see, between 1 and 10 there are just four primes, namely 2, 3, 5 and 7. Between 11 and 20 there are again four – 11, 13, 17 and 19, but after that the density gets progressively less. Between 20 and 30 there are only two, 23 and 29, and between 30 and 40 also two, 31 and 37. However between 40 and 50 there are three, 41, 43 and 47, but between 50 and 60 there are again only two, 53 and 59. From 60 to 70 there are two again, but between 70 and 80 there are three, namely 71, 73 and 79.

When two adjacent primes differ by two, as with 11 and 13 they are known as twin primes. When they differ by six, for instance 23 and 29, or 31 and 37, they are known as sexy primes – from the Latin for six. There are some cute numbers which are also prime when their digits are reversed. These are known as EMIRPS (prime spelt backwards) and include 13, 17, 31, 37, 71, 73, 79, 97, 107, 701, 113 and 311.

A STRANGE PRIME

The prime number 73,939,133 has a very strange property. If you keep removing a digit from the right hand end of the number, each of the remaining numbers is also prime. It is the largest known number with this property.

So 73,939,133 and 7,393,913 and 739,391 and 73,939 and 7,393 and 739 and 73 and 7 are all primes!

Finding new primes

Within the confines of his Paris monastery the 17th-century priest and mathematician Marin Mersenne worked diligently to find a formula for testing whether a number is prime and to discover new ones. He succeeded in coming up with the simple formula $P = 2^p - 1$ where P is a prime number already known and p is a new one. So for example $2^5 - 1$ is 64 – 1 or 63, which is prime. However there is a flaw in his theory that makes it less than perfect. For instance $2^{11} - 1$ is 2,047 which can be divided by 23, so it is not prime. A prime that 'obeys' the Mersenne formula is known, logically, as a Mersenne prime.

Over the centuries mathematicians worldwide have speculated about the way in which prime numbers become farther apart as they get bigger, on just how big they can be and whether there is a largest number beyond which there are no more primes. Euclid himself devised a method that might produce a very large prime number. If you multiply all the known prime numbers together and add 1 to the number you get, you have a sporting chance of finding a new prime. There are exceptions however, for example 30,031, which is $2 \times 3 \times 5 \times 7 \times 11 \times 13 + 1$, or 59×509.

A pattern of primes

In 1963, while doodling in his notebook during a presentation, the Polish mathematician Stanislaw Ulam noticed that when numbers are written in a spiral, prime numbers always tend to fall along diagonal lines. This was not so surprising in itself, because all prime numbers except for the number two are odd, and diagonal lines in such spirals are alternately odd and even. Much more startling was the tendency of prime numbers to lie on some diagonals more than others – and this happens regardless whichever prime you start with in the middle. There are mathematical conjectures as to why this prime pattern emerges, but none has yet been proven.

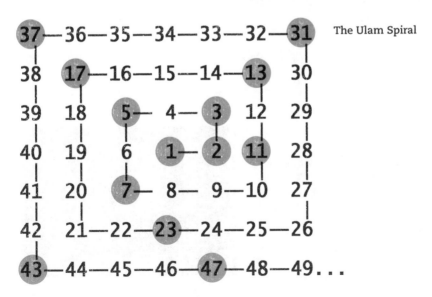

The Ulam Spiral

MAKING SHAPES WITH NUMBERS

SIMPLY PLAYING WITH NUMBERS, AS NUMBER 'ADDICTS' LIKE TO DO, CAN LEAD, PERHAPS SURPRISINGLY, TO THE SHAPES OF THE TRIANGLE, SQUARE – AND MORE.

The Greek mathematician Pythagoras significantly related numbers to shapes. It is possible to do this with simple arrangements of dots:

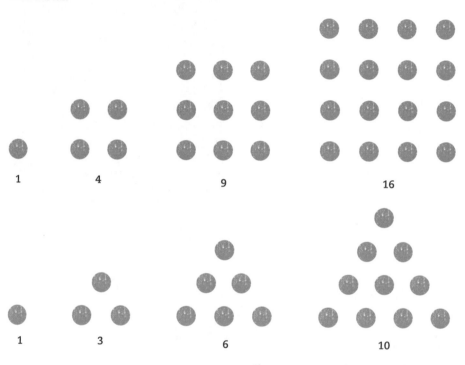

1   4   9   16

1   3   6   10

This arrangement immediately reveals the square numbers 4, 9, 16, 25 and so on. By arranging numbers in triangles, the resulting triangular numbers are 3, 6, 10, 15, 21 .... And it is interesting that when you add consecutive triangular numbers what you get is a square number. To the right is another way of laying out the answer by adding up odd numbers:

$$1 = 1$$
$$1 + 3 = 4$$
$$1 + 3 + 5 = 9$$
$$1 + 3 + 5 + 7 = 16$$
$$1 + 3 + 5 + 7 + 9 = 25$$
$$1 + 3 + 5 + 7 + 9 + 11 = 36$$

Again, the answers to the sums are all square numbers: 1^2, 2^2, 3^2, 4^2, 5^2 and 6^2.

Going higher

In a similar way, numbers can be arranged in pentagons and hexagons:

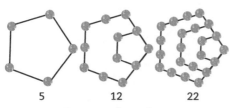

| 5 | 12 | 22 |

Pentagonal numbers

Pentagonal numbers group themselves like this, with inner pentagons fitting themselves inside the single version. As you can see the first few numbers after 1 are 5, 12, and 22, which are followed by 35, 51 and 70.

Hexagonal numbers build up in a similar way:

Here the sequence following 1 runs 6, 15, 25, 28, 45, 66, 91 …

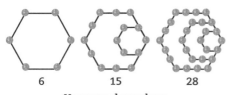

| 6 | 15 | 28 |

Hexagonal numbers

THE FAMOUS TRIANGLE

Although it had already been known in China for centuries, Blaise Pascal, the 17th-century French mathematician is famous for his triangle which he himself called the 'arithmetic triangle'.

What makes the triangle extraordinary is that while every row starts and ends with 1 each number between is the sum of the two numbers directly above it. The top row – the single 1 – is called row 0. So in row 4, the 6 is 3 + 3 and each of the 4s is 3 + 1. It was Pascal who worked out the many other mathematical possibilities that the triangle offers, notably in calculating probabilities.

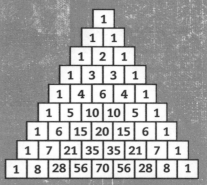

Pascal's triangle

NUMBERS – MORE DIFFERENT TYPES

MATHEMATICIANS LOVE PLAYING WITH NUMBERS AND HAVE DEVISED ALL MANNER OF LABELS AND DESCRIPTIONS FOR THEM.

Abundance and perfection

Some numbers are described as perfect, a concept brought to light by the ancient Greeks. To understand them you first need to see how a number divides. Take the number 30. Apart from itself, it can be divided by 1, 2, 3, 5, 6, 10 and 15. Adding up all these divisors comes to 42, which is bigger than the original 30. This makes 30 an abundant number. By contrast 15 can be divided only by 3 and 5, totalling 8, which makes 15 a deficient or defective number. Now try out the exercise on 28, which can be divided by 1, 2, 4, 7 and 14 – which add up to 28, making 28 a perfect number. There are not too many of these and only the first five were known by the 16th century.

Many numbers, and certainly most of the ones we use day to day, are known as rational. That is because it is possible to express them as fractions. A good example is 0.5 which can be written as ½.

Rank	1	2	3	4	5	6	7
Perfect Number	6	28	496	8128	33,550,336	8,589,869,056	137,438,691,328

Numbers can work in pairs in a way that is extremely pleasing. So-called amicable numbers, probably recognized since the time of Pythagoras, were once used in devising horoscopes. An example of such numbers are 220 and 284. The first, 220, can be divided by 1, 2, 4, 5, 10, 11, 20, 22, 44, 55 and 110, which add up to 284. Do the same for 284 and you find that the divisors add up just as neatly – to 220.

BEYOND ENORMOUS

If designated in £ sterling, 2,305,843,008,139,952,128 – which is Perfect Number 8 – would be bigger than Britain's National Debt.

Irrational numbers

Delving into more tricky territory it is necessary to go back to Pythagoras who proved that in a right angled triangle the square of the hypotenuse is equal to the squares of the other two sides. So in the triangle illustrated, $h^2 = 1^2 + 1^2$. So, by mathematical logic, h^2 must equal 2 and h itself must be $\sqrt{2}$ (the square root of 2). Unlike rational numbers, which can be expressed as a ratio of two whole numbers, $\sqrt{2}$ cannot, which is why it is called an irrational number.

While Pythagoras himself believed all numbers to be rational it was his student Hippasus who proved the existence of irrational numbers. Of all the irrational numbers, π is almost certainly the best known. However the discovery of irrational numbers did not bring Hippasus good fortune. When he drowned in the sea it was said that the gods were punishing him for defying perfection.

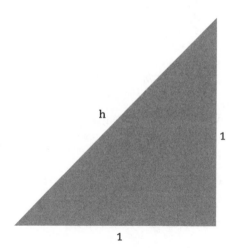

The square of the hypotenuse is equal to the squares of the other two sides

π – THE MOST FAMOUS NUMBER

THE FIRST LETTER OF THE GREEK WORD *PERIMITROS*, MEANING CIRCUMFERENCE, IS THE CLUE TO Π OR PI, THE BEST-KNOWN SYMBOL IN ALL OF MATHS. IT IS Π WHICH, WHEN MULTIPLIED BY A CIRCLE'S DIAMETER (OR TWICE THE RADIUS), GIVES THE ANSWER TO THE LENGTH OF THE CIRCUMFERENCE.

A rough value of π has been known for centuries, but first try working it out for yourself. Take a round, flat plate or tin lid and measure its diameter (D). Now take a piece of string and, with the help of sticky tape, place it all around the circumference, cutting it off as exactly as you can. Measure it to get the figure C, the circumference. Then use a calculator to divide C by D. The answer should be 3 followed by a string of numbers – if you've been accurate these will begin with a 1 or a 2. That is π or 3.14159.... a number that has now been calculated – with the help of a computer – to more than 12 million decimal places.

The scholars' work

Calculating the circumference of the circle was a problem attempted in ancient civilizations and it is even referred to indirectly in the Old Testament. Both the Egyptians and the Babylonians knew it to be a little more than three, but it was the

Archimedes

Greek mathematician Archimedes of Syracuse who, in the 3rd century BCE made the first 'proper' calculation of π which he believed to be somewhere between 223/71 and 220/70 (or 22/7), fractions which have been used as an approximation ever since and are still useful for 'good enough' calculations today. The Greeks were disappointed, however, to find that π was not a rational

number but a never-ending string of numbers in which no orderly pattern has never yet been discerned. For this reason it is called an irrational number.

In the centuries that followed mathematicians from around the world have worked to unravel π mathematically. The 5th-century Chinese mathematician and astronomer Tsu Ch'ung-chih (Zu Chongzhi) made an accurate approximation for π between 3.1415926 and 3.1415927 (355/113), which held good for the following 900 years when the Iranian Al-Kashi managed 16 decimal places. Thereafter various Europeans concentrated on the issue of π, notably Gottfried Leibniz who discovered in 1673 that:

$\pi/4 = 1 - 1/3 + 1/5 - 1/7 + 1/9 \ldots$ and so on

which, although correct mathematically, and a very elegant formula, is a very tedious means of calculation.

FIBONACCI – THE BRILLIANT NUMBER SEQUENCE

IN 1202 A BOOK WAS PUBLISHED THAT CHANGED THE WAY WE THINK ABOUT NUMBERS. ENTITLED *LIBER ABACI (THE BOOK OF THE ABACUS)*, IT WAS WRITTEN BY LEONARDO OF PISA, KNOWN MORE FAMOUSLY AS FIBONACCI, FOLLOWING HIS TRAVELS THROUGH EGYPT, SYRIA AND WHAT IS NOW ALGERIA AND WAS DIRECTED TOWARDS BOTH ACADEMICS AND BUSINESSMEN.

The Fibonacci sequence, which begins 1, 1, 2, 3, 5, 8, 13, 21, 34 ... works, as you can see so that each new number in the sequence is the sum of the previous two. It was probably known to the ancient Greeks in around 500 BCE, but it was Fibonacci who introduced it to the wider world.

Fibonacci based his reasoning on calculations of the breeding capacity of rabbits which he expressed in this way: 'A certain man put a pair of rabbits in a place surrounded on all sides by a wall. How many pairs of rabbits can be produced from that pair in a year if it is supposed that every month each pair begets a new pair which from the second month on becomes productive?'

The answer to the problem is this:

Month 1: 2 adults mature and breed. **Total:** 1 pair.

Month 2: the original 2 breed again but the offspring are not mature enough to breed. **Total:** 1 pair.

Month 3: both the first 2 adults and the first 2 offspring breed. **Total:** 2 pairs.

Month 4: the first 2 adults and the first 2 pairs of offspring breed. **Total:** 3 pairs.

Month 5: the first 2 adults and 3 pairs of offspring breed. **Total:** 5 pairs.

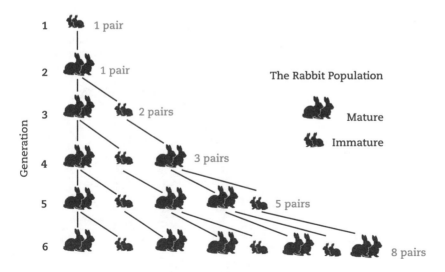

The Rabbit Population

Mature

Immature

Generation

1 — 1 pair
2 — 1 pair
3 — 2 pairs
4 — 3 pairs
5 — 5 pairs
6 — 8 pairs

Calculating the numbers of rabbits – and assuming of course, that the sexes match up conveniently and that none die – the sequence develops by addition.

Fibonacci himself did not give his name to the sequence, that was done by the French mathematician Édouard Lucas in 1877 who studied it closely in the context of primes, and who opened the door to studies of the way in which it is associated with the golden ratio (see The golden ratio). He even came up with his own sequence:

2, 1, 3, 4, 7, 11, 18 … which from the number 3 onwards follows the same rule as the Fibonacci sequence and is indeed closely related to it mathematically.

The sequence in practice

In the world around us – both natural and manmade – the Fibonacci series makes multiple appearances. Most strikingly, Fibonacci numbers can commonly be found in the natural world. In a mature sunflower head, for example, the seeds are arranged

Seed flowerhead spiral

in interlaced spirals, one set going clockwise, the other anticlockwise. The number of spirals a head contains often coincides with a Fibonacci number. In a similar way the seed containing 'pods' in a pine cone and the segments of a pineapple are arranged in pairs of spirals. These are unequal in number but often total two consecutive Fibonacci numbers such as 3 and 5.

It may well have been his observation of the Fibonacci series in nature that led Leonardo da Vinci to make the spiral his favourite design. Whether he was depicting curly hair, whirlpools or shells he drew countless spirals conforming implicitly to Fibonacci proportions.

A SPECIAL DAY

Each year, 23 November is celebrated as Fibonacci day. In American notation it is 11/23, which corresponds to the series. However the last year that was a Fibonacci number was 1597; the next will not fall until 2584.

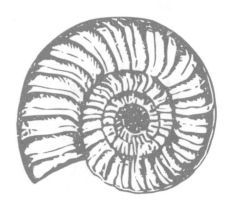

THE GOLDEN RATIO

HAVE YOU EVER WONDERED WHY SOME FACES ARE MORE ATTRACTIVE THAN OTHERS, OR WHY SOME PAINTINGS OR BUILDINGS ARE SO PLEASING TO THE EYE? ALTHOUGH WE ARE PROBABLY NOT AWARE OF IT, THE ANSWER LIES IN THE GOLDEN RATIO OR MEAN.

To find the golden ratio draw a line and divide it, as the picture shows, so that the ratio between the larger and smaller of the two parts is identical to that between the original line and the larger of its subdivisions. It is as simple as that.

BY OTHER NAMES

The golden mean is also called the golden or divine section, the medial section, the divine or golden proportion, the golden cut and the golden number.

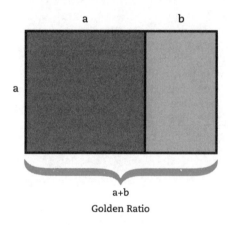

Golden Ratio

Another easy way to understand the golden ratio is to go back to the Fibonacci sequence of numbers and to see what they can do. If you divide a Fibonacci number by the one preceding it in this sequence this is what happens:

1/1 = 1.0, 2/2 =1, 3/2 = 1.5, 5/3 = 1.333, 8/5 = 1.6 ... 55/43 = 1.617

As you continue you get closer and closer to the number close to that known as the golden ratio or golden mean, which is 1.61803 followed by a string of numbers (in a similar manner to π) and is denoted by the Greek letter phi ϕ.

You also get the same result if you work out the ratio between any two numbers in a sequence in which a number is the sum of the previous two. So if you take the sequence 7, 10, 17, 27, 44, 71 .... the ratios of the last two numbers will always be 1.618 or phi.

Using or observing the golden ratio, whether intentionally or not, is one of the secrets of beauty. In the most beautiful human face the mouth and nose are positioned relative to the eyes and chin according to the golden ratio. And the perfect smile is one in which the central incisors are 1.618 times wider than the lateral ones. Similarly, proportions displayed in art and architecture – whether the creators were aware of it or not – are most attractive to the eye when they conform to the golden ratio. Measuring up paintings by Michelangelo or Mondrian, and buildings as diverse as the Great

Pyramid of Giza and Le Corbusier's Villa Stein, proves the point emphatically.

Early calculations

Ancient Greek mathematicians such as Euclid were fascinated by the golden ratio because it appeared frequently in their studies of geometry. To Pythagoras it was 'the most beautiful and pleasing proportion'. Much later the Franciscan monk Luca Pacioli explored it in his 1509 book *De divina proportione*, illustrated by Leonardo da Vinci, in which he pointed out the connections between its proportions and what he called the characteristics of God.

NATURE'S BEAUTY

The golden ratio, 1.618034 is a critical number when it comes to creating such perfect structures as the seed head of a sunflower where every seed is placed adjacent to the next by a turn represented by the golden ratio (see Fibonacci) or the shell of a nautilus or a snail.

To draw the pattern of the shell the first step is to create a rectangle whose sides are in proportion to the golden ratio. Next, the rectangle is divided into a square and a rectangle and the process repeated. From the point at which the two diagonals drawn converge it is possible to create a spiral exactly like that of a nautilus shell. The cochlea of our inner ear could be drawn in the same way, or the curl of a ram's horn.

Leonardo's Vitruvian Man

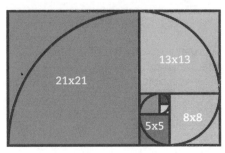

Fibonacci Spiral

NUMBERS IN USE

WHEN IT COMES TO USING NUMBERS, THE WORD AVERAGE IS USED BOTH RIGHTLY AND WRONGLY TO DESCRIBE THE PROPERTY OF A SET OF NUMBERS. THE KEY TO GETTING IT CORRECT IS TO KNOW ABOUT THREE SORTS OF AVERAGE – THE MEAN, THE MEDIAN AND THE MODE.

It is obvious to all of us that not everyone is the same height. Nor do we all share the same foot size or the same waist measurement. But if you were thinking of selling dresses or trousers, shoes, socks or tights, you would certainly want to have a range of sizes on offer. So the first question you would want to ask is: what is the average size of my buyers? What you now have to do, however, is to work out which sort of average is going to be most helpful. That is where the three measures – the mean, the median and the mode come into play.

The mean measurement

Imagine that you are buying trousers or shorts to sell and that, working in inches, the waist sizes of your regular customers might be:

AN AVERAGE JOKE

Before crossing a river a man who couldn't swim worked out that the average depth of the water was 3 feet. So why did he drown? Because in the middle of the river there was a huge pit 12 ft deep!

28, 29, 29, 30, 30, 31, 31, 31, 32, 32, 32, 32, 32, 33, 33, 33, 34, 34, 34, 35, 35, 36, 37, 38, 39, 40, 41, 43, 44, 45, 47, 48, 50, 52, 55, 56, 57, 59, 60, 65

Just looking at these numbers, it looks as if most of these people are in pretty good shape, but that there are a few with a decidedly hefty build. How does this affect what average you might arrive at?

Often when you ask for the average, people simply calculate the arithmetic mean, usually simply called the mean. This is easily obtained by adding up all the measurements, then dividing the total by the number of values – in this case 40.

Which gives the sum 1,582 ÷ 40 = 39.55

Calculating the mean is all very well but it is not necessarily helpful because there are some waist measurements, especially the numbers in the 50s and 60s at the top of the scale, that are exceptional. What is more helpful in this case is the middle or median measurement. To find it you simply choose the value placed in the list of measurements where half the values are greater and half the values less – in this case 35.

THE EASY ANSWER

If you want to find the median height of a group of 15 children line them up in height order. Then pick the eighth one along (the one in the middle) and ask them how tall they are. That will be the median, whatever the heights of the tallest and shortest.

The useful mode

For the clothes seller, however, the most useful number of all is the mode, or most common value, in this case waist size 32. Given that *mode* is the French word for fashion, you could say, in fact, that 32 is the most fashionable value. If you were going to sell only one size, you might well choose the mode. Sometimes you find that an average is bimodal – that is, there are two numbers that appear most often.

Making sense of the numbers

Looking at the numbers, and the results of the three types of average, it is obvious that the way the numbers are distributed is not symmetrical – they have the mode and the mean larger than the median. Knowing all of this has obvious practical advantages for the clothes retailer. Selling most of the mean size – rounded up to 40 – would seriously reduce your number of customers and leave you with excess stock. So you need to offer a range, concentrating on the mode – the most typical size – and the sizes to either side of it. In this case knowing the range, the difference between the smallest and largest numbers, that is 33, is not hugely helpful but it can be in other instances.

Armed with knowledge of means, medians and modes you will be well placed to question the kinds of statistics regularly presented to the public, especially when the word average is used. It could also be useful if you find yourself worried at the end of a long section of road where there was a notice announcing an 'average speed limit' of 50 mph.

Say you travelled 24 miles in 30 minutes, your average speed per minute would be $24 \div 30 = 0.8$ miles per minute. Then multiply by 60 for the number of minutes in the hour: $0.8 \times 60 = 48$. This puts you safely within the limit.

A useful measure

Looking at the way in which numbers arrange themselves around a mean is also a useful tool for analyzing everything from people's heights and weights to their incomes and spending patterns. This is measured by what is called a standard deviation or SD, or the amount of variation in a set of numbers. It is easiest to see and understand when numbers (in this case height) are converted into a graph such as the one below.

When the standard deviation is low, in which case the numbers are placed close together, the graph will be tall and thin, when it is high – meaning that the numbers are far apart – the curve will be wider and more shallow. Because the resulting curve, as here, is symmetrical around the mean then the distribution is said to be normal.

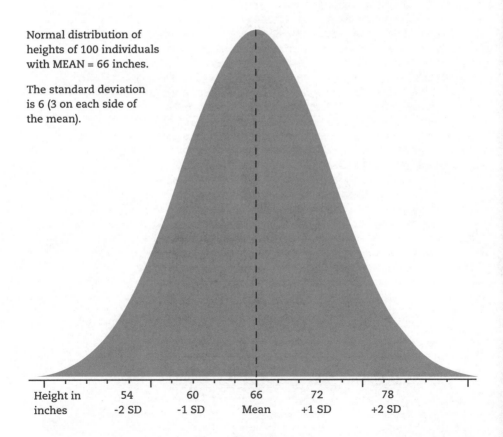

Normal distribution of heights of 100 individuals with MEAN = 66 inches.

The standard deviation is 6 (3 on each side of the mean).

Height in inches	54 -2 SD	60 -1 SD	66 Mean	72 +1 SD	78 +2 SD

THE WORLD
WE LIVE IN

There is no doubt that numbers are essential to making sense of our lives and surroundings, and of the planet we inhabit. It is not difficult to imagine how people in early societies needed to quantify the world around them, from the passing of time to the quantities of material goods, both animate and inanimate, which they used and traded. Over the centuries these systems have become ever more extensive, so that numbers have come to assist us in almost everything we do day to day.

An overview of the earth and the way in which it is mapped begin the investigation here. On a smaller scale, attention turns next to measuring lengths and weights, volumes, time and money and the history of their invention and refinement, whether based on the 10 of the decimal system or the 12 of the imperial. From the five arms of the starfish to the five petals of the wild rose, numbers also help to define the living world – including our own bodies and the way they work. Number 10 Downing Street and 1600 Pennsylvania Avenue are arguably the world's two most famous addresses, along with the fictional 221B Baker Street, home of Sherlock Holmes, all of which feature here, as do the post and zip codes that have come to define us. Travelling by road, we rely hugely on numbers for orientation and instruction, whether we are on the M25, E3 or Route 66.

At the table we can enjoy long-established food and drink brands such as Heinz 57 varieties 7 UP, and measure the alcohol we consume in well-defined units from specific bin numbers. Out shopping our clothes sizes are defined by numbers, as are such luxuries as Chanel No 5 perfume and gold and platinum jewellery with quality defined in carats. All of which adds up to a compelling mixture.

OUR PLANET EARTH

EARTH, THE THIRD PLANET FROM THE SUN, IS THE FIFTH LARGEST IN THE SOLAR SYSTEM AND, AS YET, IS THE ONLY ONE KNOWN TO SUPPORT LIFE AND TO HAVE LIQUID WATER ON ITS SURFACE. THIS IS THE EVER-CHANGING ENVIRONMENT EACH OF US SHARES WITH MORE THAN SEVEN BILLION OTHER HUMANS.

Some 4.5 billion years ago the earth was formed from a swirling mass of gas and dust and now circles the sun at 107,180 km/hour or 66,660 mph once every 365.3 days. It has just a single moon. These are just a few more of the earth's vital statistics:

Minimum distance from the sun:
147,000,000 km (91,340,000 miles)

Maximum distance from the sun:
152,000,000 km (94,450,000 miles)

Diameter at the equator:
12,756 km (7,926 miles)

Surface area:
509,600,000 km^2 (197,000,000 miles^2)

Average temperature: 22°C (71.6°F)

Tilt and the seasons

Day and night exist because the earth rotates on its axis approximately once every 24 hours, but because the earth is tilted on its axis at an angle of 23.44° from the vertical, there are only two days a year – the vernal equinox on 21 March and the autumnal equinox on 22 September when day and night are of equal length. Equally the tilt accounts for our northern hemisphere seasons, and the summer and winter solstices on or around 21 June and 21 December in the northern hemisphere.

On land

Some 250 million years ago the seven continents we know today were once joined together in one vast landmass known as Pangaea. Over time the tectonic plates on which the land is placed have moved, creating the shape of continents and oceans we know today and, from collisions between plates, many of our mountain ranges.

Oceans and seas

Added together, the world's five oceans – the Pacific, Atlantic, Indian, Southern and Arctic – contain 97 per cent of all the water on earth and cover about 71 per cent of its surface. They form one continuous mass of water and contain the world's longest mountain range. This mid-ocean ridge, stretches some 50,000 km (30,000 miles) from the Arctic to the South Atlantic. At its southern end it branches into two, extending east into the Indian Ocean and west into the Pacific. The deepest point in the oceans is the Mariana Trench in the Pacific, measured at 10,920 metres (35,826 ft).

HURRICANE OR TORNADO?

The difference between these two powerful storms depends on size and wind speed. While a hurricane is a large revolving storm with a diameter up to 160 km (100 miles) and winds exceeding 119 km/h (74 mph), a tornado or twister is up to 400 m (¼ mile) across with winds up to 300 km/h (200 mph).

OUTSTANDING FEATURES
Continent by continent these are:

Location	Highest mountain	Longest river	Largest lake	Largest island	Highest waterfall
Europe	Mt Elbrus, Caucasus, 5,663 m (18,580 ft)	Volga 3,690 km (2,293 miles)	Aral Sea, Kasahkstan 65,500 km² (40,700 miles²)	Great Britain 21,8041km² (13,484 miles²)	Uitgård, Norway 800m (2,625 ft)
Asia	Everest, Tibet/ Nepal, 8,848 m (29,029 ft)	Yangtze, 5,540 km (3,442 miles)	Caspian Sea, 394,299 km² (245,000 miles²)	Borneo, Indonesia, 736000 km² (457,327 miles²)	Hannoki-no-taki, Japan, 497 m (1,600 ft)
Africa	Kilimanjaro, Tanzania, 5,894 m (19,337 ft)	Nile, 6670 km (4,145 miles)	Victoria, 69,500 km² (43,185 miles²)	Madagascar, 590,000 km² (366,608 miles²)	Tuela, South Africa, 856 m (2,808 ft)
North America	Mount McKinley, Alaska, 6,194 m (20,322 ft)	Mississippi-Missouri, 5,970 km (3,710 miles)	Superior, 82,350 km² (51,170 miles²)	Greenland, 2,173,600 km² (1,350,607 miles²)	Yossemite, California, 739 m (2,425 ft)
South America	Cerro Aconcagua, Argentina, 6,969 m (22,864 ft)	Amazon, 6,448 km (4,007 miles)	Titicaca 8,135 km² (3,140 miles²)	Tierra del Fuego, 49,935 km² (1,9280 miles²)	Angel Falls, Venezuela, 979 m (3,212 ft)
Oceania	Kosciuzho, 2,229 m (7,312 ft)	Murray-Darling, 3750 km (2,330 miles)	Lake Eyre, 9,580 km² (5,953 miles²)	Australia, 2,941,526 km² (1,827,773 miles²)	Wallaman Falls, Australia, 300m (984 ft)
Antarctica	Vinson Massif, 5,140 m (16,864 ft)				Blood Falls, 14 m (46 ft)

Measuring powerful forces

Among the powerful forces on earth are those that create earthquakes and volcanoes. Although more sophisticated measurements are now used, earthquakes are still measured on the Richter scale, named in 1935 for its American developer Charles F. Richter. On this scale each whole number increase in magnitude represents a tenfold increase in measured amplitude and an increase of about 31.6 times of the energy released. To date, the top five most powerful are:

Date	Location	Magnitude
22 May 1960	Valdivia, Chile	9.4 – 9.6
27 March 1964	Prince William Sound, Alaska	9.2
26 December 2004	Indian Ocean	9.1 – 9.3
11 March 2011	Pacific Ocean, Japan	9.1
4 November 1952	Kamchatka, Russia	9.0

The 2004 earthquake also resulted in a massive tsunami, giant ocean waves up to 30 metres (100 ft) high that killed more than 230,000 people from 14 countries.

Volcanoes, caused when gas or molten lava is ejected from the earth's surface, are measured by their Volcanic Explosivity Index (VEI), based on the volume and height of material that erupts. Small eruptions, classed as grade 1 or gentle occur daily in Hawaii, the earth's most active volcanic region. A cataclysmic eruption, of 4 VEI can be expected every 10 years and a megacolossal one of VEI 8 only every 10,000 years.

These are the volcanoes estimated as most deadly since the eruption of Mount Vesuvius in AD 79 believed to have killed more than 13,000 people as it buried Pompeii and Herculaneum.

Volcano	Year	Estimated death toll
Mount Tmabora, Indonesia	1815	71,000
Krakatoa, Indonesia	1883	36,000
Mount Pelée, Martinique	1902	30,000
Nevado del Ruiz, Colombia	1985	23,000
Mount Unzen, Japan	1792	15,000

LINES ON THE MAP

TODAY, ANY ORDINARY SMART PHONE CAN, VIA GPS, GIVE YOU THE COORDINATES OF YOUR EXACT LOCATION WITHIN SECONDS – A FAR CRY FROM THE EARLY DAYS OF MEASURING AND MAPPING OUR PLANET.

It was while working at the library in Alexandria that the scholar and polymath Eratosthenes of Cyrene, (276–195 BCE) first measured the earth's circumference without even leaving home. And he was remarkably accurate, being only 320 km (200 miles) within the modern measurement of 40,075 km (24,901 miles). How he began was to compare the altitude of the midday sun at two places placed north-south that were a known distance apart, namely Alexandria and Syene which today is Aswan.

Key to Eratosthenes' calculation was his knowledge that in Syene the sun was directly overhead at noon on the summer solstice. Using a vertical rod called a gnomon he recorded the angle of elevation of the sun at noon in Alexandria by measuring the length of the rod's shadow on the ground. This gave him the numbers he needed to calculate the angle of the sun's rays, which was 7° or approximately 1/50 of the circumference of a circle. Assuming the earth to be exactly spherical, (which it isn't quite), and knowing the distance to Syene, he calculated that the earth's circumference was 50 times that distance.

It was probably around the era of the Greek scholar Homer in the 8th century BCE that the concept of the equator, the imaginary line dividing the earth into northern and southern hemispheres, originated. The word was almost certainly used before 1610 when it was integral to the phrase *circulus aequator diei et noctis* meaning the 'circle equalizing day and night'.

North and south

In measuring and recording latitude, the equator is taken to be 0° and 90 lines or parallels are drawn above and below it, as far as the poles, making 180 in all. The North Pole has a latitude of 90° north or +90°, while that at the South Pole is 90° south or -90°. A single degree of latitude, or arcdegree, covers about 111 km (69 miles). The chief lines of latitude have familiar names – the tropics of Cancer and Capricorn and the Arctic and Antarctic Circles.

Although the margins are small, the exact positions of the Arctic and Antarctic Circles are not constant because the tilt of the earth changes by 2° over a period of 40,000 years as a result of tidal forces created by the moon's orbit. This means that the Arctic Circle is annually moving north at around 15 m (49 ft). As of 5 May 2018 it has been at 66°33'47.1" north. Similarly the Antarctic Circle is now at 66°33'47.1". These two circles closest to the poles mark the points beyond which, to north and south, the sun can stay above the horizon for 24 hours – the midnight sun – at or near the solstices.

The Tropics of Cancer and Capricorn

Some 2,000 years ago, when these lines were first named, the sun was visible in the constellations of Cancer and Capricorn at the summer solstices, the points in the year in which the sun is directly overhead, although today the situation is totally different and continues to change. These geographical markers are also moving – at around 15 m (49 ft) a year towards the equator. So the Tropic of Capricorn is now at 23°26'12.9" south of the equator and the Tropic of Cancer the same distance north of it.

The problem of longitude

Compared with latitude, which proved relatively easy to calculate, longitude posed many problems from its conception, especially at sea where there are, literally, no landmarks. In the 2nd century BCE the mathematician Hipparchus made longitude calculations by comparing an absolute time taken at a prime or zero meridian running through Rhodes with the 'real' time in known locations.

From the time of Ptolemy (c AD 100–170), maps were produced bearing lines of longitude or meridians. The first 'modern' European to suggest a solution was the Italian financier, explorer and cartographer Amerigo Vespucci who used as his guide the relative positions of Mars and the moon. Galileo, too, addressed the issue, showing in 1612 that the positions of the moons of Jupiter could be used as a universal clock.

Until the 18th century sailors had relied heavily for navigation on lines of latitude, and on dead reckoning, a calculation based on a ship's speed over a certain

Harrison's chronometer

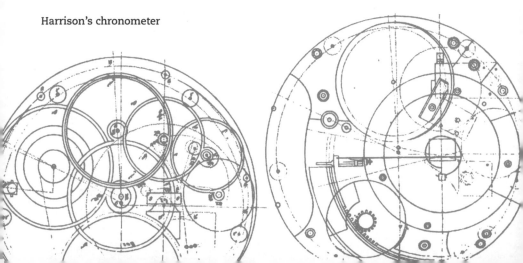

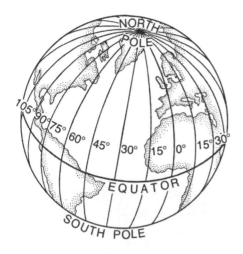

made the most significant advance. Although never awarded the top prize his total payments from the Board totalled £23,065.

From the early days, geographers set the map measurements to their own specifications. For Eratosthenes, his prime meridian of 0° longitude ran through Alexandria, while Indian scholars set it in Sri Lanka. In China it was Bejing and in Japan Kyoto. By the mid 19th century it became clear that a prime meridian of 0°, set in a specific place, needed to be established, from which measurements of +180° eastward and -180° westward could extend.

Britain, the world's major colonial power at the time, proposed that it should run through Greenwich, which despite being derided as a 'dingy London suburb' became accepted at a conference in Washington in 1884, ahead of glamorous locations such as Paris, Mecca and the Pyramid of Giza. And indeed it runs today through the Royal Observatory in Greenwich.

time and distance. This was not accurate enough to prevent either shipwrecks or voyages extended beyond the bounds of safety. In 1714, following a tragedy in 1707 off the Isles of Scilly, the British government (noting also the effects on trade) established a Board of Longitude announced a prize for 'such person or persons as shall discover the Longitude'.

Most famous of the many entrants and money winners was the clockmaker John Harrison whose marine chronometer, which he improved in a series of versions, was the device that

The world's time zones

The Washington conference also agreed to divide the globe into 24 time zones, each representing 15° of longitude and with time 'beginning' at Greenwich Mean Time or GMT. Since the earth completes its rotation in 24 hours, the day appears to start earlier if you are east of Greenwich, or later if you are to the west. The local time within a time zone is defined by its difference or offset from Coordinated Universal Time (UTC). UTC time changes one hour forward and backward one hour for every 15 degrees east or west of the prime meridian.

For many countries whose boundaries fall within 15° degrees of

THE SIZE OF THE PRIZE

The 1714 Act offered prizes escalating in value according to accuracy, from £10,000 for determining longitude within 1 degree to £15,000 for a value within 40 minutes and £20,000 (around £2.7 million today) for a value within 30 minutes.

The novelist Jules Verne anticipated the international date line in his 1873 adventure *Around the World in Eighty Days* in which Phileas Fogg, having thought he had lost his wager discovered that he had won his bet by gaining a day.

Countries such as the USA and Canada, however, were so big that it was deemed necessary to have several different time zones over the breadth of the country (see right).

Also established at the Washington Conference was the International Date Line (UDL). Although based essentially on the meridian of 180° longitude,

a time zone the whole country works to one standard time. In the UK, this practice started with the advent of railways in the first half of the 19th century. Before this, when every city set its clock to local time by the sun, significant discrepancies occurred.

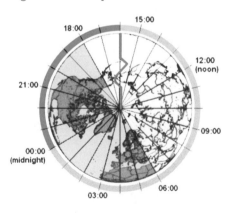

- —— International Date Line
- ▇ Monday
- ▒ Tuesday
- ▢ Night/Day

THE FAMOUS BOUNDARY

The 49th parallel north is renowned as the line of latitude which, for some 3,500 km (2,175 miles) marks the border between the USA and Canada. In 1714 the Hudson Bay Company first proposed a border between its land and that owned by the French, but it took until 1818, and an intervening war between America and Britain (who now owned the land to the north), for the solution to stick.

In the years following the setting of the border, indigenous people still held territories on each side of the line. They nicknamed it the Medicine Line because of its seemingly magical ability to prevent US soldiers from crossing.

In Europe the 49th parallel runs some 15 km (9 miles) north of Paris, through Charles de Gaulle airport, and in Germany through Karslruhe where it is marked with a stone and a painted line in the Stadtgarten.

and running through the middle of the Pacific, this deviates west or east in many places, often for political expediency, as in the separation of islands belonging to the USA and Russia. There is also an enormous 'bite' which allows certain island nations to be first to welcome the new day (or New Year).

TIME ZONES AROUND THE WORLD

Some notable zones and anomalies include:

USA and Canada: Eastern, Central, Mountain and Western zones, respectively 5, 6, 7, and 8 hours behind GMT.

India: a single zone 5½ hours ahead of GMT.

Pakistan: one zone 5 hours ahead of GMT. But although a substantial part of Pakistan is east of the westernmost part of India, it has a time zone implying that it is to the west.

Singapore: 8 hours ahead of GMT. If you travel from Singapore to Jakarta, mostly eastwards, you would expect the local time to be later than in Singapore. But it is one hour earlier! This is because Indonesia, despite being so broad, has standardized time zones.

Portugal: uses GMT.

France, Italy, Germany and countries in the west of mainland Europe: 1 hour ahead of GMT. Spain is the exception because Madrid is west of London but shares the time zones of Paris, Rome, Berlin and so on. This makes evenings very light in Madrid, which is maybe why its residents dine so late in the evening.

Chile and Argentina: both are 3 hours behind GMT. Chile is so far east that it should probably be 5 hours behind, equal with east coast USA, but equality makes travel and trade much easier. As a result it has dark mornings and long, light evenings.

MEASURING THE WORLD

NUMBERS ARE ALL IMPORTANT WHEN IT COMES TO MEASURING THE DIMENSIONS OF OUR PLANET AND EVERYTHING IT IN. FROM MEASURING COOKING INGREDIENTS TO CHECKING OUR WEIGHT, IT IS THE NUMBERS THAT COUNT - LITERALLY.

The human body itself provided early people with a convenient means of measurement, and the ten digits of the hand almost certainly gave rise to the counting system used in Mesopotamia and the Iranian plains from around 3000 BCE. In ancient Egypt, counting was essential when it became necessary to

A RULER FOR A RULER During the rule of Tutankhamun (c.1332–23 BCE) the royal treasurer Maya employed a hardwood cubit rod (now in the Louvre in Paris) divided into 28 units, each measuring 1.86 cm (about ¾ in). Smaller divisions are marked along the side, while on the upper surface each division is inscribed with hieroglyphs relating to individual gods, beginning with Ra.

calculate the size of grain stores and to record numbers of cattle (see Numbers and counting).

Ancient civilizations, including Egypt, Greece and Rome, made extensive use of the cubit, the distance from the elbow to the tip of the middle finger, although its value could range from 44 to 64 cm (17 to 25 in). The human stride is an approximation for a yard (36 in or 91 cm) while the foot was, for the Greeks and the Romans (who called it the *pes*) directly equivilant to human foot length. The Romans then divided this into 12 inches or *unica*, each the width of the thumb. The fathom 1.8 m (6 ft), used for measuring the depth of the ocean, was originally based on the span of a man's two outstretched arms.

The imperial system
It was from the Romans that the British imperial system of measurement, based on the number 12, evolved, which may

even have been derived by adding the four fingers on the hand to the three 'sections' in each finger created by the joints. And of course a year of 12 months composed of 12 × 2 hours in the day, each made up of 12 × 5 minutes, had already been long recognized (see Inventing the calendar). Certainly 12 is a more flexible number mathematically compared with 10, being divisible by 1,2,3,4, 6 and 12, and was also used in Britain from Roman times for the currency.

Until the adoption of decimal currency in 1971, Britain traded in pounds made up of 20 shillings, each composed of 12 pence. The penny was further divided into four farthings. Money was referred to as LSD, an acronym for *librae*, *solidi*, and *denarii* – Latin for pounds, shillings and pence. For distance, the imperial measurement was the mile, named from the Latin *mille passum* or thousand paces made up of 5,000 *pes*. It was not until around 1500 that the 'old London' mile was defined as eight furlongs, which at that time was 625 feet, making a mile 5,000 feet. Then, under a 1593 statute during the reign of Elizabeth I, an additional 280 feet were added.

Going metric

Until the 18th century a whole range of measures was used worldwide for specifying distance. Although the French cleric Gabriel Mouton had suggested in 1670 that the dimensions of the earth be used for standardizing measurements, it was not until 1789 and the French Revolution that Mouton's notion was converted from theory to practice. The result was the metre, being one ten-millionth of the distance between the North Pole and the Equator. Ten years later a platinum rod measuring exactly

MILES AT SEA

Until the early 16th century, navigation at sea was done purely by eye. The nautical mile was first proposed by the scientist Edmund Gunter, who in the early 17th century used the lines of latitude to calculate distance and proposed the nautical mile as one minute or 1/60 of one degree of latitude or 6,080 feet. The current international definition, precisely 1,852 m, was not agreed on until 1929, and not adopted by the USA until 1954. To travel at 1 knot is to move at 1 nautical mile per hour.

EVOCATIVE TERMS

Some old fashioned measures are still in use – others survive as little more than curiosities:

Hand: employed in ancient Egypt and still used for determining the height of horses from the ground to the withers (the top of the shoulders). Originally the breadth of the palm, including the thumb, but now standardized at 4 inches (10.16 cm).

Furlong: Originally the length of a furrow in a ploughed field, $\frac{1}{8}$ of a mile, equalling 220 yards or 201.168 m. The furlong is still used as a horse racing measure in most parts of the world, except for Australia, which turned metric in 1972. A furlong equals 40 poles.

Rod, pole or perch: In Medieval times, ploughing was done with up to four pairs of oxen, controlled with a stick long enough to reach all eight animals. This was the rod, pole or perch, a length of 5½ yards, 16½ feet, $\frac{1}{320}$ of a mile or, in metric, 5.0292 m. All were originally used for determining the acreage of land, and a 'perfect' acre of 43,560 square feet is a rectangle or strip of land measuring 220 by 22 yards or 40 by 4 rods.

Chain: The length of a cricket pitch, or 22 yards (20.1 m), a term used since 1620. There are 10 chains in a furlong and 4 poles in a chain.

League: Defined in Ancient Rome as 1½ miles (now 2.2km) the league on land is 3 miles and at sea is 3 nautical miles, which is 3.452 miles or 5.556 km.

Guinea: In old British money, one pound one shilling. Once widely used in pricing luxury items it is still used for buying and selling of horses and persists in the names of horse races such as the 1000 and 2000 Guineas.

one metre was first housed in France's National Archive and all other divisions calculated by multiplying or dividing by 10. Deriving from the metre came the litre, or 1,000 cubic centimetres, and the gram which is the weight of 1 cubic centimeter of water.

From 1840, the metric system was officially adopted in France and quickly copied all over Europe. Today it is the worldwide standard in the sciences. Modern Britain, despite beginning metrication in 1965 still stubbornly uses a mix of measurements while the USA continues with its own version of the imperial system.

Hot or cold?
Only in the 17th century did measuring temperature became a practical possibility. Galileo had devised a rudimentary device in 1592, but it was the Italian noble, the Grand Duke of Tuscany, Ferdinand II who in 1641 created a sealed alcohol-filled device that was the prototype of the modern mercury-filled version. The first temperature scale was devised by the German physicist, Gabriel Fahrenheit, who originally set 0 as the lowest temperature (from a mixture of ice, water and sea salt), and 96° as normal body temperature. As thermometers became more refined, the Fahrenheit scale was standardized as 32° for the freezing point of water, 212° for boiling water and 97° for normal body temperature.

It was Anders Celsius, a Swedish astronomer who in 1742 first devised the so-called Centigrade scale with 0° for freezing and 100° for boiling water. Since then scientists have established other scales such as the Kelvin in which 0 is the lowest possible temperature – absolute zero, which is equivalent to -273.15° Celsius or -459.67° Fahrenheit.

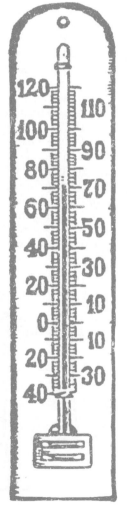

TEMPERATURE RECORDS

-89° Celsius (-218°F) is the lowest recorded temperature on earth at Vostok, Antarctica on 21 July 1983.

56.7° Celsius (134°F) is the highest recorded temperature on earth at Furnace Creek, USA on 10 July 1913.

A MATTER OF WEIGHT

WEIGHT IS ESSENTIAL IN MATTERS OF TRADE, AND FROM AT LEAST 6000 BCE BOTH THE EGYPTIANS AND BABYLONIANS USED SIMPLE SCALES TO WEIGH THEIR GOODS.

The philosophers of ancient Greece were intellectually engaged by the concept of weight. While Plato believed it to be the way in which objects 'sought their kin' to Aristotle it was the means by which the 'natural' order was restored and to Archimedes it was the opposite of buoyancy. The first practical definition: 'the heaviness or lightness of one thing compared to another, as measured by a balance' was the pronouncement of Euclid.

The word pound probably originates from the Roman *pondo*, a weight of around 12 oz (340 g), although the abbreviation lb comes from the *libra*, which was the basic unit of weight which the Romans brought to Britain. After 268 BCE this became standard, measuring some 5,076 English grains, or 0.722 pounds avoirdupois (in metric 0.329 kg). The *libra* (meaning scales or balance) was used most specifically for weighing gold and silver and for all business transactions. The *unica*, from which the word ounce derives, was one twelfth of a *libra*.

Pounds of many sorts

The pound has been defined in many different ways over the centuries but in the UK Weights and Measures Act of 1963 was officially defined as 0.453 592 37 kilograms exactly. In Britain the most ancient is the Tower or King Offa's pound dating to AD 757 and measured against a piece kept in the Tower of London. This pound was based on the weight of 120 Arabic silver dirhams, each worth two pence. Such coins have been excavated from Offa's Dyke, the old fortification separating England and Wales. The Rochelle pound, named from the French port was also known as the Moneyers' pound (dating from the Saxon era) and the Easterling pound. It may have been known in Germany but was certainly commonly used for trade throughout the Hanseatic League. It remained legal until 1527. Then there was the London pound, composed of 16 ounces, which although used by the League never became a legal measure.

For jewels and medicines

From the 9th century, both jewellers and apothecaries used the Troy pound, possibly named from the trading centre of Troyes in France, and composed of 12 troy ounces and 5,760 grains, which in today's metric measurement is exactly 373.2417216 grams. Although no longer officially recognized troy ounces (12 to the pound) are still used by precious metal markets. Each troy ounce contains 20 pennyweight (dwt), each dwt

containing 24 grains. The value 240 dwt to the pound is the origin of Britain's old money system.

The apocetharies' pound also contains 12 ounces and is equivalent to 0.37 kg or 0.82 avoirdupois pounds. Each ounce contains 8 drachms, each drachm 3 scruples and each scruple 20 grains. This breakdown made it possible to measure very small quantities of powerful medicines and remained legal in both Britain and the USA until 1858.

The standard system

The pound recognized today, and still used in the USA, is the avoirdupois version, dating to the 13th century. Later authorized as standard by both Henry VIII and Elizabeth I, it was adopted by statute in 1340 and again in 1350 by Edward III. It is named from the old French *aveir de peis*, meaning goods of weight, which would have been measured before being traded, notably wool, hence the nickname 'wool

pound'. In the USA it was defined by the Mendenhall Order of 1893 as 2.20462 pounds to the kilogram, but revised a year later to a more accurate 2.20463334 pounds.

The original avoirdupois pound or *livre* consisted of 16 ounces (*onces*), each composed of 16 'parts'. There were 14 pounds in a stone or *pere* and 26 stones in a woolsack. From the Tudor era, 28 lb composed a quarter, 112 lb a hundredweight (cwt), and 20 cwt a ton. In the US, however, a hundredweight or short cwt is 100 lb and a ton or short ton 2,000 lb or 20 US cwt. The pre-metric British units are known as the long hundredweight and ton. For ease and clarity, however, the metric weights adopted in France (see Measuring the world) are ideal. The metric tonne is simly 1,000 kg.

SETTING THE STANDARD

To back up his statutes Edward III commissioned standard weights, now held at the Westgate Museum in Winchester. These weighed 7 lb (the wool-clip); 14 lb (stone); 56 lb (4 stone) and 91 lb (¼ sack or woolsack) and remained in use for more than 200 years.

WEIGHT OR MASS?

Ordinarily, the words weight and mass are used synonymously to express weight or heaviness, but scientifically there is a distinct difference between the two – which all depends on gravity. This concept can be traced back to medieval times when weight of an object was measured either as its static value or *pondus*, while its *gravitas* altered as it fell.

Mass simply measures the amount of matter in an object, and is measured in our everyday units of kilograms, pounds and tons. Vitally, mass remains the same wherever an object is located and is the same on earth as it is on the moon.

Weight, however, is technically the force an object experiences when it is pulled downwards by gravity and is measured in Newtons (N) named for the great scientist Isaac Newton and based on his second law of motion. At sea level the weight of a 1kg bag of flour is the same as its mass, but were it on the moon, where the pull of gravity is about ⅙ of that on Earth, it would weigh ⅙ less.

To calculate the weight of the 1 kg bag of flour in Newtons you need to multiply the mass by the acceleration due to gravity, which is 9.8 metres per second squared: On Earth the answer is 1kg × 9.8 m/s^2 = 9.8 Newtons.

On the Moon it is 1kg × 1.6 m/s^2 = 1.6 Newtons.

Mass = 1kg
Weight = 9.8 N

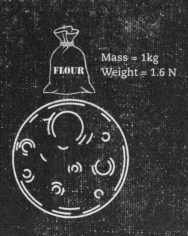

Mass = 1kg
Weight = 1.6 N

BY VOLUME

WHILE WEIGHT WAS TRADITIONALLY RELATIVELY EASY TO MEASURE ONCE SCALES WERE INVENTED, VOLUME WAS MUCH MORE TRICKY, SINCE BASKETS OR JARS COULD VARY HUGELY IN SIZE, AND REMAINED SO FOR CENTURIES.

In the ancient world, measuring grain and wine were two essentials of trade, demanding both dry and liquid measures. One early Greek unit was the *cotyle* or *cotyla*, which was not standard but varied between 210 and 330 ml in metric measurements. In ancient Rome, both liquid and dry volume measurements were carried out using jars or amphora. The basic unit was the amphora quadrantal, equivalent to one cubic *pes* or Roman foot. One eighth of the amphora quadrantal was the congius or half-pes while the sextarius was ⅙ of a congius. If the Roman foot was 296 mm, then the amphora quadrantal was around 25.9 litres and the sextarius around 540 ml.

By the gallon

The origin of the gallon, possibly named from *gellet*, the Old English for bowl, originated in Britain to measure the volumes of wine and beer. In America it also measured corn. The smallest measure was the wine gallon, which also measured other liquids including brandy, mead, cider, oil and even honey. It was later also known as Queen Anne's gallon from a statute of 1707, which standardized it as 231 cubic inches (3.79 litres). This wine gallon became the US gallon, where it has been standard since the early 19th century.

The beer and ale gallon, which became the imperial measure, was eventually adopted officially in Britain

JUST A PECK

Introduced in the 14th century as a measure for flour, the peck is a quarter of an imperial bushel, that is, 2 imperial gallons (8 imperial quarts or 9.092 litres). It makes a memorable appearance in lyrics from the 1950 musical *Guys and Dolls* which begins:

I love you, a bushel and a peck!

A bushel and a peck, and a hug around the neck!

A hug around the neck, and a barrel and a heap

A barrel and a heap, and I'm talkin' in my sleep.

in 1824 as 282 cubic inches (4.62 litres), when all other forms of gallon were abolished. At this date it was based on the volume of 10 lb of distilled water weighed in air with brass weights and in an environment of 67°F, and with the air pressure measured at 30 inches of mercury.

The corn or dry gallon, or Winchester gallon, is intermediate between those for ale and wine, measuring around 268.8 cubic inches or 4.405 litres. It is named from the town in England where the standard examples were kept after

Henry VII regularized volume measures in 1495. It is an eighth of the Winchester bushel which was originally a cylinder 8 in deep with a diameter of 8½ in.

Make mine a pint

Although still used when ordering drinks at the pub, the pint is almost a redundant measure in Britain since the arrival of metrification, a process that began in earnest from the mid 1960s, but is still a legal measurement (equivalent to 568 ml) for draught beer and cider, and for milk sold in returnable glass bottles. What you get in other countries may well vary. In Germany a stein is 500 ml, while in America it is likely to be a smaller 473 ml. In the US it is common for alcoholic drinks to be sold in fifths, each of which are around 20 per cent of a US gallon.

The barrel business

Barrels are still used for measuring dry goods from salt to cranberries, but barrel measurements are nowhere more critical than in the oil industry, where worldwide the barrel, officially 42 US gallons (about 159 litres or 35 imperial gallons) holds sway. For conversion to

COMPARISONS AND CONVERSIONS

The way traditional measures have come to differ between the imperial quantities adopted in Britain (although now superseded by metric quantities), and the USA

versions are easy to understand when compared directly. The figures have been rounded to two decimal places. For measuring cooking ingredients America uses cup measures, a cup being ¹⁄₁₆ of a US gallon.

Unit	Imperial ounces	Imperial pints	Millilitres	Cubic inches	US ounces	US pints
Fluid ounce	1	¹⁄₂₀	28.41	1.73	0.96	0.060
Gill	5	¼	142.07	8.67	4.80	0.30
Pint	20	1	586.26	34.68	19.22	1.20
Quart	40	2	1136.52	69.36	38.43	2.40
Gallon	160	8	4546.09	277.42	153.72	9.60

The pint gets its name from the Old French pinte and also possibly from the Latin pincta or painted, a reference to the divisions customarily painted on the side of a container to indicate its capacity. In France, and also Qubec, 'une pinte' is an imperial quart, while a pint is 'une chopine'.

metric 1 cubic metre is taken to equal 6.2898 oil barrels. For trading, barrels are expressed on stock markets in Mbbl (a thousand barrels) or MMbbl (a million barrels). The designation goes back to the Drake Well, America's first oil well, drilled in 1858, when barrels once used for whiskey, beer or fish were put to use to hold this liquid gold. Of these, the 40-gallon whiskey barrel was the most popular and available, but it quickly became obvious that a standard measure was required. The 42-gallon barrel was set as being 40 gallons, plus 2 gallons 'in favour of the buyer'.

Oil production is commonly expressed in barrels per day (abbreviated as BPD, BOPD, bbl/d, bd or b/d), where 1BPD is 0.0292 US gallons per minute. Variations in the density, expressed as API (American Petroleum Institute) are also taken into consideration, since these can affect the volume. Two thirds of the world's oil prices are set by the standard of Brent Crude which has an API gravity of 38.05 compared with West Texas Crude at 39.6 and Dubai Crude at 31.

MORE ABOUT MONEY

MONEY IS, IN ESSENCE, A PARTICULAR MEANS OF COUNTING, BUT ONE LINKED INEXTRICABLY TO VALUE. THE POUNDS, EUROS OR DOLLARS IN OUR POCKETS HAVE A LONG HISTORY.

Some 4,000 years ago, Mesopotamian scribes scratched onto clay tablets the values of key goods such as wool, barley and oil compared with a standard weight of silver. This metal was a kind of money, but precious metals were not used as 'real' money until the 7th century BCE when coins of electrum, a natural alloy of gold and silver, were struck in standard weights and stamped with images to indicate their value.

During the Roman occupation, Britain used the rigid monetary system of their colonizers. The basic unit was the aureus, equal to 25 denarii. One denarius was originally worth 10 bronze asses, but the ass was replaced in 89 BCE with the sestertius, worth a quarter of a denarius. And in AD 312 the solidus replaced the aureus.

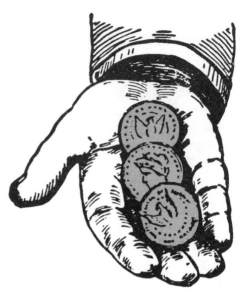

The penny, named from the Germanic word for 'pledge' was introduced by both the ruler Egbert of Kent in the 8th century and the Mercian king Offa. Very soon 240 silver coins or sterlings were made from a pound of silver – and from this all Britain's modern money derives.

On paper

Although the Chinese had invented paper money as early as the 7th century the first European versions were the Swedish fixed value notes of 1661. It was the need for money to fight the French in 1694 that prompted not only the foundation of the Bank of England but first hand written 'promisary notes'. By 1745 printed notes were being issued with face values ranging from £20 to £100, exchangeable for their face value in gold. £1 and £2 notes followed in 1797.

The dollar story

It was Bavaria, not America, where the dollar originated, in the city of

FIRST OF MANY The original ruler to issue coins bearing his name was the Persian emperor Darius I in the 5th century BCE. His gold daric with a standard weight of 8.4g (⅓ oz) was equal in value to 20 silver sligos.

ENSURING THE VALUE

Because it was easy to debase coinage valued for its weight by making counterfeits with copper or other low value metals in the core, or by shaving pieces off the edges, from 1663 British coins were made with milled edges. To ensure the providence of paper money the Bank of England began impressing notes with watermarks as early as 1697.

Joachimsthal. Here, in 1518, silver from the nearby mines was minted into *thalers*, each with a standard weight of 29.2 grams or just a little over an ounce. These became standard all over Europe. In the new world the Spanish dollar, made from mines in locations such as Mexico, became commonly used but it was only after the American Revolution of 1792 that the dollar, now so called, was standardized as 27.0 grams of silver (0.952 oz).

Paper money had been circulating for a century or more when, during the America Civil War greenbacks, so named because they were printed in green on the reverse side, were issued as demand notes from 1861–62. In 1863, the American Congress set up the national banking system and granted the US Treasury permission to issue authorized bank notes which, although legal tender were not backed up by gold or silver, only the government's credibility.

Integrating economies

The euro was born as the currency of the European Union as a result of member states seeking economic stability and integration. After a decade of preparations it was finally launched on 1 January 1999. Only after three years of trading with so-called 'book money' was the euro launched for real. On 1 January 2002, 14 billion notes and 52 billion coins were ready for use in 12 countries: Austria, Belgium, Finland, France, Germany, Greece, Ireland, Italy, Luxembourg, the Netherlands, Portugal and Spain. By 2018 there were 19 countries using the euro but notably not the United Kingdom.

NAME THAT COIN

American coins have nicknames that reflect their history:

1 cent – the penny – named from the English coinage used before the Revolution.

5 cents – the nickel – first dubbed the half dime, was originally made of silver or copper and nickel alloys but made solely of nickel after 1883.

10 cents – the dime – originally officially the '*disme*', an old French word for tenth when introduced in 1792 but called the dime from day one.

25 cents – the quarter – an obvious name.

INVENTING THE CALENDAR

SINCE THEIR INVENTION, CALENDARS HAVE BEEN USED TO FIX THE OCCURRENCE OF IMPORTANT EVENTS THROUGHOUT THE YEAR, AND TO RECKON TIME IN ADVANCE. FROM ANCIENT TIMES CALENDARS RELATED TO EASILY OBSERVED NATURAL PHENOMENA SUCH AS ANNUAL HARVESTS AND RELIGIOUS FESTIVALS.

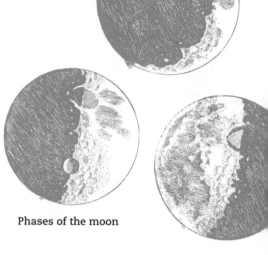

Phases of the moon

In ancient Egypt, the year was originally divided into three seasons – the flooding of the Nile, seed sowing and harvest. In time this became the 12-month year we know today, based on the moon's cycles. Cycles of the moon, lasting some 28 days, allowed months to be defined with ease, but solar cycles, which follow the seasons more faithfully, were much more useful for agriculture.

Moon and sun

Unfortunately for the early calendar makers, the cycles of the sun and moon do not synchronize well, and the peoples of the ancient world wrestled with this inconsistency. A lunar year (consisting of 12 lunar cycles, or lunations, each 29½ days long) lasts for only 354 days, 8 hours, while a solar year lasts approximately 365¼ days. After three years, however, a strictly lunar calendar would already have diverged from the solar calendar by 33 days, or more than one lunation.

The moon's phases have nonetheless remained a popular way to divide the solar year, although a 365¼-day year doesn't lend itself to equal subdivision. To compensate for the difference in the solar and lunar year, calendar makers began adding extra days or months. The solution for the ancient Greeks was to vary the lengths of months to be either 30 days (full months) or 29 days (hollow months). However the Greek astronomer Hipparchus (2nd century BCE) measured the time taken for the sun to travel from one equinox to the same equinox again, then calculated the year length to be $\frac{1}{300}$ of a day less than 365.25 days, that is 365 days, 5 hours, 55 minutes, 12 seconds, or 365.24667 days.

Adding accuracy

When Julius Caesar took power in Rome in 46 BCE the calendar was three months out of synch with the seasons. The solution, devised by the Alexandrian astronomer Sosigenes, was to add a day to the month of February every fourth year – what we now call a leap year. This calendar, introduced by Julius Caesar and named 'Julian' took effect in 45 BCE, shortly after the Roman conquest of Egypt, and became the predominant calendar throughout Europe and in European settlements in the Americas and elsewhere.

Even with the addition of the leap year, the Julian calendar still gained one day in every 128 solar (tropical) years

and by 1572 the calendar was still wrong by 11 days. As a result Pope Gregory XIII ordered a revision so that in 1582, October 5 became October 15. In addition, it was decreed that there should only be 97 leap years in every 400, which is why there is no leap year in a date that can be divided by exactly 400. Even so we are now nearly three hours ahead of the time set by the Gregorian calendar.

Acceptance of the change did not happen quickly or universally. Only in 1752 did the British Parliament eliminate 11 days between 3 and 13 September when Wednesday 2 September 1752 was followed by Thursday 14 September. This caused some disquiet, but particularly with business people who believed that they were being cheated of revenue. Russia originally adopted the change in 1917 and China delayed until 1949.

A confusion of dates
On 23 April 1995, UNESCO celebrated the first World Book Day, a date chosen because it was believed that both Miguel Cervantes, the author of *Don Quixote*, and William Shakespeare had died on 23 April 1616. However, because of the quirks of the calendar this assumption was mistaken; by this time Spain had switched to the Gregorian calendar, while England had not, making Shakespeare's 'real' death date 3 May 1616. What is more Cervantes was buried on 23 April having died the previous day.

From France: a revolutionary system
In an attempt to remove all religious and revolutionary influences from the calendar, and as part of the move to decimalization the French Republican or Revolutionary Calendar was created and used from late 1793 to 1805, and for 18 days by the Paris Commune in 1871. The year began at the autumn equinox and the 12 months were divided

Julius Caesar

into three ten-day weeks or *décades*. Replacing Sunday, every tenth day or *décadi* was a day of rest and celebration. At the year end five or six additional or complementary days were added to align to the solar year. Every four years was marked as a leap year. (See also time and circle).

Days in the week

The week of seven days dates back to ancient civilizations but has only a loose connection with other aspects of the calendar. Certainly there is a link with the seven days of creation described in the Old Testament book of Genesis, from which the importance of marking rituals every seventh day may arise.

Seven remains important in Judaism, although in Hebrew the days of the week are assigned numbers not the names of gods, festivals, elements or planets, except for Saturday, *Yom Shabbat* which is the Sabbath.

The idea of the seven-day week was probably first conceived by the Babylonians for whom the number seven had a mystical significance associated with the seven heavenly bodies: the Sun, Moon, Mars, Mercury, Jupiter, Venus and Saturn. This is reflected in the names we now give to the days of the week, which come from the Graeco-Roman tradition and link strongly to its deities.

Name	Sunday	Monday	Tuesday	Wednesday	Thursday	Friday	Saturday
Derivation	Sun	Moon	Mars	Mercury	Jupiter	Venus	Saturn
Greek link	Helios	Selene	Ares	Hermes	Zeus	Aphrodite	Kronos
Latin link	Sol	Luna	Mars	Mercurius	Iuppiter	Venus	Saturnus

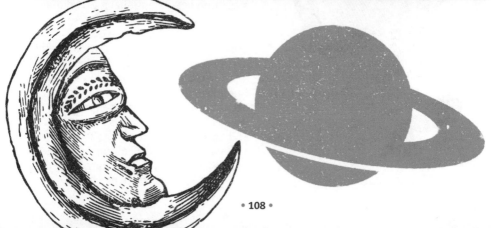

CALENDARS OF MANY KINDS

The calendar has taken on different forms through history, including these notable examples:

The Babylonian calendar had 12 months and years grouped into 19-year cycles. To increase its accuracy one month was repeated in year 17 of each cycle.

The Muslim calendar is the only purely lunar calendar in widespread use today with a year of 354 days. Religious celebrations, such as Ramadan (which advances by 11 days each year), may thus occur at any date of the Gregorian calendar.

The Jewish calendar of 12 months runs between new moons but with an extra 13th 'embolismic' month added when the year is out of synch with the seasons.

The Maya had three different calendar systems. The first had 365 days consisting of 18 months of 20 days, plus 5 days. The second was a 260-day cycle or *tzolkin* of sacred days connected with a 365-day cycle in a Calendar Round of 52 years. The third, the Long Count, was based on a combination of 360-days (a *tun*) plus a number system based on 20, with 20 *tuns* equaling 7,200 days.

TIME AND THE CIRCLE

FROM THE MOMENT OF BIRTH OUR LIVES TICK BY AT 60 SECONDS TO THE MINUTE, 60 MINUTES TO THE HOUR AND 24 HOURS TO THE DAY. BUT HOW DID SUCH A SYSTEM ORIGINATE, AND HOW DOES IT RELATE TO THE SIMPLE CIRCLE?

It was probably the Egyptians who first divided the day into sections by erecting simple sundials and measuring the way in which the shadows that were created moved around in a circle each day. By around 1500 BCE they had devised 12-part calibrations to indicate the hours between sunset and sunrise. As these developed, summer hours were measured as longer than winter ones. The 12 hours of night were divided according to the rising and setting of 12 stars, with another three of the 36 significant stars recognized in the heavens classified as belonging to the twilight.

The ancient Greeks took the Egyptian system to further levels of accuracy and between 147 and 127 BCE Hipparchus came up with the proposition of dividing the day into 24 hours of equal length based on the measurements taken at the equinoxes. Dividing each hour into 60 and then 60 again was almost certainly an inheritance from the astronomical observations of the Babylonians who used base 60 as their means of calculation.

Dividing the circle

It was his attempts to come up with a system of latitude that led the Greek astronomer Eratosthenes (c 276 to 194 BCE) to divide the circle into 60 sections, but it was Hipparchus who set the lines of latitude around the globe and also

the lines of longitude, each of which encompassed 360 degrees. Following on from him, Ptolemy divided the 360 into 60 minutes, each then divided into what he called 'second minutes' or, today, simply seconds (see Lines on the map).

Only in the 15th century were clocks invented with hands that circled the clock face, but they were not sophisticated enough to show minutes until a century later. Today time is measured at the atomic level, a second being defined as about 9 million oscillations of a caesium atom.

DECIMAL TIME

In their desire to make everything metric French revolutionaries attempted to create a workable system with the day divided into 10 decimal hours, each made up of 100 minutes and with 100 seconds to the minute. Like the decimal calendar it lapsed into disuse after only a few decades.

THE LIVING WORLD

FROM THE FLOWER OF A DAFFODIL TO THE ARMS OF A STARFISH AND THE LIFE CYCLE OF THE CICADA, NUMBERS REVEAL SOME FASCINATING INSIGHTS INTO THE PLANTS AND ANIMALS WITH WHICH WE SHARE THE PLANET.

The world of plants

For flowering plants, it is their seeds that divide them into two distinct groups. Within the seed are one or two seed leaves or cotyledons, which develop ahead of the true leaves. Typical of those that have just one seed leaf (the monocotyledons) are the members of the lily, iris and orchid families, and all the grasses and bamboos. Beautiful as they are, these are just a tiny proportion of flowering plant world; the majority is held by the dicotyledons, whose seeds contain two seed leaves.

When plants grow and develop, their leaves and flowers also reveal numerical qualities. Many leaves, for example, are divided into smaller leaflets in characteristic patterns. So a clover leaf has three leaflets while the leaves of the orchid tree *Bauhinia* has two. Four leaflets is a key characteristic of plants such as the wood sorrel, *Oxalis*.

Horse chestnut

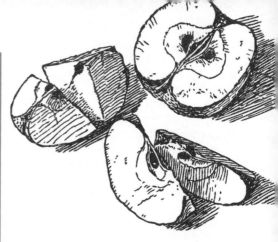

LUCKY NUMBERS

Numbers associated with certain plants can possibly affect your fortunes:

• The four-leaved clover has long been associated with good luck while a two-leaved one, put in a shoe was, for an unmarried girl, a means of ensuring a meeting with her love.

• An ash leaf with nine leaflets, held in the hand, is said to be another way of conjuring a meeting with the love of your life.

• A nine-pea pod, hung over the door was a way of inducing a lover to cross the threshold.

When leaflets are set along opposite sides of a leaf stalk odd numbers of leaflets, as in the ash, *Fraxinus*, are most common, but *Sweitenia*, the mahogany, has an even number. There are yet more complex arrangements, as in *Mimosa* and ferns, but when leaflets create hand-like shapes as in the horse chestnut (*Aesculus hippocastanum*) leaflets are generally an odd number, usually five or seven.

A flower's petals also follow some number rules that can be useful as rough guides to identification. As a rule, monocotyledons have petals arranged in multiples of three, although some may be fused together, as in a daffodil's trumpet. Typically the crucifers, which includes the brassicas (cabbages), have flowers with four petals arranged, as their name suggests, in a cross shape, while roses and their relations – in their simplest form – have five petals. Five petals is also standard in the figwort family, which includes *Buddleia*, the butterfly bush.

One is the number of seeds in fruits such as the plum, peach and almond. In apples and pears the number depends on the number of seed producing 'pockets' or carpels that form the 'core'. Apples and pears have five, and each can contain more than one seed. In pods like beans and peas – which can have from 3 to 20 peas inside – the number depends on both variety and crucially on the plant's health and its growing conditions.

The animal world

Throughout the animal world, counting appendages helps to give names to many creatures. Humans, of course, have two legs and two arms but share a four-limbed form with many other mammals and also other creatures with backbones – snakes being a notable exception. Of the five digits on our hands, our four-finger movements are made remarkably dexterous by our opposable thumbs, a trait shared by our primate relatives.

The five-digit pattern repeats itself throughout the natural world but millennia of evolution have created distinct variations on the theme such as today's single-toed horse, descended from a small five-toed ancestor. The horse, with the zebra and the donkey, are all odd-toed creatures or ungulates, as are the three-toed rhinoceros and the tapir, which has four toes on its forelimbs but three on the hind limbs. By contrast, in even-toed ungulates only the third and fourth toes of the original five still exist. Deer, camels, and many domestic animals including cattle and sheep are all like this.

For the birds
When it comes to birds, three and four are the most common numbers of digits on the feet, while the 'hands' embedded in birds' wings are believed to have evolved from the second, third and fourth digits of the hands of their dinosaur ancestors. A four-toed foot, with one of the four facing backwards, is typical of songbirds, which habitually perch when resting. In birds that climb tree trunks, such as parrots and woodpeckers, the arrangement is more even, but one digit is markedly longer than the others.

Many legs – no backbone
Distinguishing between the plethora of invertebrates often comes down to counting. These are just some examples:

• **Insects** – typically have six legs and, if winged, four wings except for the Diptera (flies), which are two-winged.
• **Arachnids** – including the spiders and scorpions – have eight legs. Orb weave spiders have eight similar eyes.

ESSENTIALS BY TWO AND FOUR
The DNA that makes every living thing unique is in essence a remarkably simple structure. It consists of a pair of spiralling polynucleotide strands joined by a sugar (deoxyribose) a phosphate and pairs of bases which combine two by two in specific pairs – adenine with thymine and cytosine with guanine.

The two-winged horsefly

• **Cephalopods** – cuttlefish and their close relations have eight tentacles.
• **Starfish** – usually have five arms but the number can vary. An unusual species named *Labidaster annulatus* can have as many as 50.
• **Shrimps, crabs, lobsters** – and other crustacean members of the order aptly named the Decapoda – have ten legs.
• **Ladybirds** – can be identified by counting their spots. The 7-spot is the most common type in Britain but a 14-spot type also lives here. Other ladybird varieties can have 2, 10 or 12 spots.

The Cicada

The amazing cicada story

The prime numbers 13 and 17 take on special significance for the cicadas of the Americas, notably those of the genus *Magicicada*. These jumping insects, renowned for their choruses, have a most extraordinary life cycle and are named from their almost miraculous behaviour.

Once the male and female cicadas have mated, the female quickly creates a cut in the bark of a tree twig where she lays her eggs. These duly hatch into immature forms or nymphs, which drop to the ground and begin burrowing with their strong front legs to reach the tree roots whose sap they feed on. Now they go through a series of pre-adult transformations before finally excavating exit tunnels. Once they emerge, they shed their final external coverings and begin to 'sing' as adults.

While most cicadas take two to five years to reach adulthood, the *Magicicada* spend either 13 or 17 years underground and emerge en masse creating a magnificent spectacle and a deafening sound. So why this long lapse? And why prime numbers? The answer seems to be that the prime number cycle helps the cicadas avoid predation from creatures with much shorter life cycles – say six or eight years.

DID YOU KNOW?

• The sloth exists in two forms, one with two toes, the other with three.

• The beauty of nature often depends on the golden ratio or mean (see The golden ratio).

• All the even-toed ungulates digest their food in multiple stomachs.

• Some of the first living things on earth had just a single cell – and today's world is teeming with single-celled organisms – animals, plants, fungi and bacteria.

THE HUMAN BODY

OF ALL THE LIVING CREATURES ON THE PLANET WE HUMANS ARE ARGUABLY THE MOST REMARKABLE. FOR DESPITE BEING 60 PER CENT WATER, WE HAVE BRAINS THAT ENABLE US TO INVENT EVER MORE SOPHISTICATED WAYS OF COMMUNICATION AND TO CONTROL OUR ENVIRONMENT. SOME OF THE BODY'S MANY VITAL FUNCTIONS CAN BE DESCRIBED IN NUMBERS.

Every day the 37 trillion cells composing our bodies perform the tasks that keep us alive. In addition the body is host to over 100 trillion bacteria, many of them essential helpers in digestion and metabolism. Vital organs such as heart and brain, liver and pancreas, lungs and kidneys, hands and feet come singly or in pairs.

The skeletal framework

Making up the body's framework is a skeleton of 206 bones, 29 of which form the skull, the protective case for the brain, eyes and ears. Of these all are fused together except for the lower jaw or mandible. Below it are the 26 spinal vertebrae. During childhood, 5 bones in the lower back fuse to form the sacrum. Shielding the heart and lungs are the 25 bones that comprise the rib cage and sternum.

The remaining bones comprise the pectoral girdle, arms and hands (64 bones) and the pelvis, legs and feet (62 bones). The 27 bones in the hand and 26 in the foot are arranged to maximize mobility. Each thumb and big toe contains a pair of bones, the remaining digits and toes have three bones each. Eight nugget-shaped bones comprise the firm but flexible wrists while the ankles are kept strong with just two bones.

Clothing the skeleton are some 650 voluntary muscles, which not only allow the body to move but, as in the case of abdominal muscles, help to protect vital organs. Many of these work in pairs, as in the upper arm. When the biceps contracts to raise the forearm the triceps relaxes.

Heart and blood

The single human heart is divided into four chambers, two atria above a pair of ventricles. As its muscles go to work, contracting some 100,000 times a day, it beats, when the body is resting, at about 70 times a minute. When exercising, anything up to 130 beats a minute is a safe maximum.

As it beats the heart continuously pumps some 5.7 litres (10 pints) of blood through 96,500 km (60,000 miles) of blood vessels, leaving the body's living pump from the left ventricle through the aorta, which measures about 2.5 cm (1 in) across.

Every 0.001 ml (microlitre or mcL) of blood usually contains between 4.7 and 6.1 million red blood cells in men and between

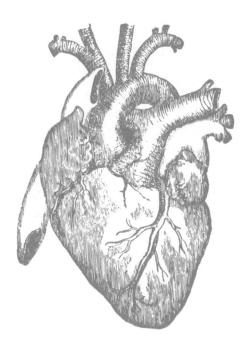

cubic feet or ft³) of air each day. While inhaled air contains 21 per cent oxygen and just 0.04 per cent carbon dioxide, exhaled air contains 16 per cent oxygen but 4 per cent of carbon dioxide.

Of our two lungs, the right is the broader with three lobes; the smaller left lung has only two lobes. Within the lungs are minute sacs or alveoli – 700 million in each lung – connected to a blood capillary network. It is here that the exchange of gases takes place. And without lungs we would be unable to speak or sing. As we vocalize, sound is produced by vibrations of the vocal cords in the larynx as air passes through them.

Digesting the figures

The food that fuels our bodies is digested in what is essentially a long, muscular tube that is ten times longer than the height of the body from head to toe. Anatomically it is divided into the mouth, oesophagus and the stomach, with a capacity of up to 2 litres (3½ pints), which leads into two major sections: the small intestine, which is about 6 m (20 ft) long, and the large intestine, which has a larger diameter and is about 1.5 m (5 ft) long. During its 24 to 36-hour passage through the system, food is digested with the help of a variety of secretions and absorbed through the folded surface of the intestines which, in the small intestine alone, measures as much as 350 square metres (1,148 sq ft).

Every minute about 1.45 litres (2½ pints) of blood flow through the liver, the organ which, at any moment, contains 13 per cent of the body's total blood volume. Its tiny lobules, numbering from 50,000 to 100,000 work as processing

4.2 and 5.4 million in women. It is these corpuscles that carry oxygen to the tissues and the waste product carbon dioxide back to the lungs for ejection. The manufacture of each red blood corpuscle, which takes place in the bone marrow, takes approximately 90 days and its lifespan is about 120 days. The various white blood cells, the keys to our disease resistance, including antibody production, are fewer in number but equally important. On average they total between 4,500 and 10,000 per mcL, but their count increases significantly when we are fighting off infection.

The breath of life

Without even thinking about it we breathe in and out between 15 and 18 times every minutes of our lives during which we shift some 14,000 litres (500

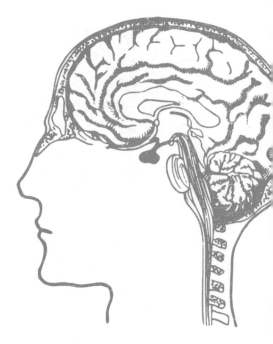

COUGHS AND SNEEZES

It is no wonder that coughs and sneezes spread diseases. A single cough ejects 3,000 droplets of moisture at the rate of 80 km/h (50 mph) but a sneeze is much more violent, ejecting as many as 40,000 droplets at up to 322 km/h (200 mph.)

plants, making bile to aid fat digestion, storing glucose in the form of glycogen, breaking down proteins into substances that include urea which is then disposed of in urine and sweat and neutralizing toxins.

Once every hour all the blood in the body passes through the kidneys about 20 times. Here it is filtered and a whole variety of waste products, including some water, are removed. Urine, the resulting fluid, is produced at about 1.45 litres (2½ pints) a day. This is made possible by around a million minute filtration units, the nephrons, contained in each kidney.

Control systems

Brain, nerves – and more than 200 hormones – comprise the body's control systems, operating 24/7 whether we are awake or asleep. The adult brain, containing over 10,000,000,000 neurons (nerve units) has a volume, on average, of 1,260 cubic centimeters or cm³ (500 in³) in men and 1,130 cm³ (445 in³)

women. Of its three major areas the largest is the cerebrum (of which the cerebral cortex is the outer layer). Divided into two lobes, linked by a nerve bundle, the corpus callosum, it is the centre of everything from memory to sensation. Below it are the cerebellum, responsible for coordinating movement and balance, and the brain stem which connects the brain with the spinal cord and controls, unconsciously, essential activities such as breathing and digestion.

Emerging from the underside of the brain are 12 cranial nerves many of which link to sensory organs. Others control finely coordinated muscle movements such as those involved in speech and facial expression. Extending from the brain is the spinal cord measuring about 45 cm (18 in) long in men and around 43 cm (17 in) in women. As well as channelling messages to and from the brain it acts independently to process reflex actions such as the knee jerk. Messages between cells are passed across gaps or synapses with the aid of chemical neurotransmitters. The system is speedy: each transmission takes between one thousandth and three hundredths of a second allowing signals to travel at up to 360 km/h (225 mph).

The essential covering

Skin, the largest body organ measures about 2 square metres (21 sq ft) in a medium-sized adult. Of its two major layers, the upper one, the epidermis, is the thinner varying from 0.1 mm on the face to a protective 1 mm (0.04 in) on the soles of the feet. Skin cells are constantly shed and removed at a rate of 4 kg (9 lb) per year. The dermis below contains blood vessels, sweat glands, hair follicles and receptors for touch, temperature and pain. Unique

NUMBERS IN OUR MOUTHS

Human teeth normally come in exact numbers, which for an adult are:

8 incisors

4 canines

8 premolars

12 molars, including 4 wisdom teeth.

Children gradually acquire their 20 milk teeth during their first 3 years, 10 on top and 10 on the bottom. There are 8 incisors, 8 molars and 4 canines.

ridge patterns on the skin, between 0.2 and 0.4 mm wide, and shared only by identical twins, are most prominent on the fingers and toes.

Overall every body bears around 3 million hair follicles each with muscles attached. A third of these are on the head. Every day individual hairs will grow about 0.3 mm per day and about 80 will be shed. Even when we are not active our sweat glands generate about 1 litre (1¾ pints) of salty sweat in 24 hours; its purpose is to help regulate body temperature and assist in removing waste products. Nails are also a product of the skin. Fingernails increase in length at about 36 mm (1⅖ in) a year but those on your dominant hand grow faster. Toenails grow at only around 12 mm (½ in) annually.

OUR AMAZING SENSES

The power of our sense organs can be summed up in some extraordinary numbers:

Eyes:
■ The retina at the back of the eye contains 125 million light-sensitive rods for black and white vision and 5 million cones for colour vision.
■ Six muscles control the movement of each eyeball, which makes 50 tiny flickering movements every second. These are essential to sight.
■ When awake we produce 1.2 ml (0.042 fluid oz) of protective tears a day.

Ears:
■ Most people's ears can detect sounds between 0 and 120 decibels.
■ Pain and damage are risks above 100 decibels, lower than the sound of an aircraft taking off.
■ 25,000 sound receptor cells are clustered in each ear.
■ The eardrum is about 8 mm (³/₈ in) in diameter.
■ Balance is controlled with the help of fluid-filled semi-circular canals, three in each ear.

Nose:
■ People with the most acute sense of smell can distinguish at least 10,000 different odours.

■ Two patches of tissue, each measuring less than 2.5 sq cm (1 sq in) contain the 50 million receptor cells responsible for smell.
■ The nose detects 7 different basic types of scent: camphoraceous, musky, floral, peppermint, ethereal, pungent and putrid.

Tongue:
■ The tongue detects 5 kinds of taste: salty, sweet, bitter, sour and umami (essentially the meat-like taste of monosodium glutamate).
■ The number of taste buds in an adult tongue ranges from 500 to 10,000. Each survives only a few days.
■ Each taste bud contains 50 to 150 taste receptor cells.

Skin:
■ A single finger may have 100 Pacinian corpuscles which are stimulated by pressure.
■ Touch organs are differently distributed. A finger can distinguish points 0.25 mm (¹/₁₀ in) apart; on the thighs the distance is 75 mm (3 in).
■ The skin's cold receptors start working when skin surface temperature drops below 35°C (95°F). They are most stimulated at 25°C (77° F). Hot receptors start working when the skin surface rises above 30°C (86°F) and are most stimulated at 45°C (113°F). Above this, pain receptors take over to help avoid damage.

New life

Approximately every 28 days until the menopause a sexually mature woman's ovary releases an egg ready to be fertilized. During intercourse a fertile male ejaculates between 2 and 5 ml of semen (about a teaspoonful), totalling between 200 and 500 million sperm. If a sperm enters the egg, making conception successful, it then takes 38 weeks for a baby to become fully formed.

In the cells of the new human (except eggs and sperm) are 23 pairs of chromosomes composed of DNA. In each pair, one chromosome originates from the mother, the other from the father.

Within 30 hours of conception the 23 chromosomes from each parent fuse together in the Fallopian tube. It can take 6 days for the cluster of dividing cells, the blastocyst, to embed itself in the lining of the uterus. Within 4 weeks the heart will begin to beat and by 8 weeks the fetus will have recognizable limbs. By 22 weeks all the body systems are established and, with medical support, could survive.

MEASURES OF HEALTH

Of all the regular health measurements, among the most useful are blood pressure and body mass index (BMI).

Blood pressure measures the efficiency of the heart and circulation and is expressed in two numbers, for example 130 over 80. Ideally the reading should consistently be between 90 over 60 and 130 over 85. If it is higher than this then your heart is working harder than it should.

The top number, the systolic pressure, records the pressure in your arteries whilst your heart muscle is contracting, the lower one, the diastolic pressure, is the pressure between beats.

Body mass index is a measure of weight. To find it you need to divide your weight by your height squared. Using kilograms and metres makes this simple:
Say you are 1.6 metres tall and weigh 65kg then your BMI is:
$65 \div 1.6 \times 1.6 = 25.39$
Since a normal BMI is between 18.5 and 24.9 this would indicate that you were slightly overweight.

A NUMBER FOR YOUR HOME

GIVING HOUSES A NUMBER IS THE OBVIOUS WAY TO MAKE THEM EASILY FOUND BY THE POSTMAN, DELIVERY DRIVERS AND VISITORS. HOWEVER THE WAY IN WHICH NUMBERING IS ALLOCATED VARIES FROM PLACE TO PLACE AND COUNTRY TO COUNTRY.

The first numbering schemes for homes date largely to the 18th century, when postal systems were burgeoning, but the first recorded were in central Paris in 1512 with the aim of determining property ownership. And in 1720 Prague introduced a numbering system to enable the authorities to pinpoint the homes of potential Jewish conscripts.

European systems

In London, the first houses to be numbered were in Prescot Street, Whitechapel, in 1798. By mid-century Vienna, Madrid and many other European cities had numbering systems, although consistency could certainly be lacking. In 1780, for example, Craven Street off the Strand in London had three sets of numbers.

It was only in 1855, with the passing of the Metropolitan Management Act, that house numbering in Britain became organized and centrally controlled. While it had been the custom to allocate numbers consecutively up one side of a street then down the other, odd numbers were now designated on one side of the street (usually the left leaving the town centre) and even numbers on the other.

Around the world

Systems similar to those in Britain and dubbed 'European style' are common throughout the continent but there are exceptions and embellishments. In Portugal, new developments are given *lote* (plot) numbers on original plans, which continue to be used after the buildings are inhabited. In Berlin and Hamburg older streets still use an anticlockwise 'horseshoe' system, with numbers starting on the right side of the street and running sequentially up one side and down the other so that the highest and lowest numbers are opposite each other.

In Slovakia, the Czech Republic and other countries in central Europe, houses always have two numbers, at least in towns and cities. In Brno, for example, a white on red sign bears the land registry or unique descriptive number – the *cislo popisné*. White on blue is used for the second sign, the reference number or *cislo orientacni*, which is the number of a house in any particular street.

Australia and New Zealand generally use the European system but in Australia numbers will start again from 1 when a significant statutory boundary is crossed. In rural districts a farm 4,400 metres (2.7 miles) from a road, on the right hand side, would be numbered 440. In Japan, cities are divided into numbered zones and houses assigned a number according to the order in which they were constructed. Both are indicated on the signage.

In Latin America the usual numbering system is the same as in Europe – except for Venezuela which identifies its building by names, not digits. In remote habitations near highways it is the kilometer distance on the highway that determines the house number. In the USA and Canada European numbering is also usual but on very long roads numbers can be over 1000. A mile marker is also employed, so a house numbered 556200 on Florida's Overseas Highway is 55.6 miles (89 km) from the 0 mile marker in Key West.

DUAL NUMBERING

In America's grid cities like New York an address will contain two numbers, as in 8 East 51st Street. It is also usual for addresses to increase by 100 at each cross street, so if an address is sited eight blocks north of a city's centre or base point it will be numbered in the range 800 to 900.

ADDRESSES IN FICTION

SOME FICTIONAL ADDRESSES ARE AS FAMOUS AS REAL ONES – AS THE LOCATIONS OF THE CHARACTERS SHERLOCK HOLMES, HARRY POTTER AND PADDINGTON BEAR PROVE WITHOUT DOUBT.

'We met the next day as he had arranged and inspected the rooms at No.221B Baker Street, of which he had spoken at our meeting. They consisted of a couple of comfortable bed-rooms and a single large airy sitting-room, cheerfully furnished and illuminated by two broad windows.' Thus the most famous of all numbered fictional addresses made its debut in Arthur Conan Doyle's A Study in Scarlet, first published in Beeton's Christmas Annual of 1887, although the author makes it clear elsewhere that Sherlock Holmes and Dr John Watson had been there since 1881. Certainly they continued their deliberations at 221B until 1904.

But, as one might expect in a good detective story, 221B is itself something of a mystery for in Conan Doyle's day, numbers in London's Baker Street (known then as Upper Baker Street, north of Marylebone Road) extended only into the 100s. It was not until the 1930s that more numbers were added and 221 was included as one of eight included in a large Art Deco House called Abbey House, the home of the Abbey Road (now Abbey National) Building Society. The company quickly became overwhelmed by correspondence addressed to Mr Sherlock Holmes.

Only in 2002, when the company vacated the building, were letters redirected to the nearby Sherlock Holmes Museum, opened in 1990 to replicate the novels' atmosphere and trappings. But although it has the number 221B emblazoned on it, this is in fact number 239; 221B still does not exist. Replicas of 221B have also been constructed at a hotel in Meiringen, Switzerland, near the Reichenbach Falls, scene of the famous battle between Holmes and Moriarty, and at Lucens, also in Switzerland.

ON SET

Number 12 Picket Post Close in Bracknell, Berkshire, was chosen in 2000 as the location for the Dursley home for shooting the Harry Potter films. In 2016 the house was put on the market for £475,000 having been bought six years earlier for £290,000.

FOR THE FANS

In the USA Holmes aficionados can visit the 221B Room in Wilson Library at the University of Minnesota, a reconstruction that boasts the world's largest collection of Sherlock Holmes ephemera.

The Potter Home

Number 4 Privet Drive, Little Whinging, Surrey, England is renowned as the address of Vernon and Petunia Dursley, their son Dudley and Harry Potter, son of Lily, Petunia's late sister. Advising Harry on the magical protection that the house affords, Dumbledore (who delivered him there after his parents were murdered) reassures Harry that: 'While you can still call home the place where your mother's blood dwells, there you cannot be touched or harmed by Voldemort ....' JK Rowling admits that she unconsciously made 4 Privet Drive a more spacious up-market version of a house she lived in as a child in Winterbourne, near Bristol, and to have chosen four because it always struck her as 'rather hard and unforgiving'.

A bear's residence

When creating the children's favourite, Paddington Bear, author Michael Bond amalgamated his parents' address at Winser Drive, Reading with his own in Arundel Gardens, Notting Hill, to come up with 32 Windsor Gardens, just off Harrow Road, not far from Maida Vale. It was 1958 when Paddington first moved in with the Brown family, having travelled from 'darkest Peru' before being discovered at Paddington Station. There is a real version of this address in West London, often visited by disappointed tourists who discover that the space is occupied by a block of flats with no number 32.

A DARK HISTORY

TWO PARTICULAR ADDRESSES HAVE NOTORIOUSLY SINISTER CONNECTIONS. ONE IS NOW A MUSEUM, THE OTHER HAS BEEN DEMOLISHED AND DISAPPEARED.

A place of safety?

On 10 May 1940, five days after the bombing of Rotterdam, Dutch forces capitulated to the Germans and their country became occupied territory. On 1 December that year, Otto Frank moved the offices of his spice company to Prinsengracht 263, Amsterdam, using the front of the building for storing goods and a middle section for milling.

As the months progressed, life for the Jewish residents of the city became increasingly dangerous. For her 13th birthday on 12 June 1942, the last before she and her family went into hiding, Anne chose for her gift the notebook that became her diary. In it she vividly described the 'secret annex' or *Achterhuis*, well hidden by adjacent houses, with accommodation for staff and family above a warehouse. But on 4 August 1944, all those 'imprisoned' were betrayed and sent to Nazi concentration camps. Only Otto Frank survived and initiated the publication of Anne's diaries as their co-author.

Far from glamorous

Today, Notting Hill is one of London's most desirable and expensive districts, but in the late 1940s and early 1950s, when John Reginald 'Reg' Halliday Christie moved into a flat at 10 Rillington Place, this was a slumland. Other tenants of the building included Timothy Evans, his wife Beryl and their baby Geraldine. Following the murders of his wife and baby by Christie, Evans was wrongly convicted and subsequently hanged on 9 March 1950.

Fifteen years later, following a posthumous pardon, the Evans case effectively led to the suspension of capital punishment for murder in the United Kingdom. In all at least eight people, including Christie's wife Beryl, were unlawfully killed at 10 Rillington Place. The house was renovated during the 1960s and 70s but in 1978 the entire building was knocked down and the name of the infamous street remains only in the historical record.

THE STREETS OF POWER

IN BOTH BRITAIN AND THE UNITED STATES THE RESIDENCES OF POLITICAL LEADERS HAVE ADDRESSES SO NOTABLE FOR THEIR NUMBERS THAT THESE HAVE BECOME PART OF THE VOCABULARY.

Numbers 10 and 11

Originally built in 1581 by Sir Thomas Knyvet, a member of parliament and favourite of Queen Elizabeth I, 10 Downing Street was dubbed a 'vast, awkward house' by William Pitt the Younger when he took up his first term in residence in 1782. By then there had already been a great deal of alteration and the house that exists today was originally three houses – a stately mansion 'the house at the back' overlooking St James's Park, a town house and a small cottage. It is the townhouse, one of a number built by the Irish born American Sir George Downing between 1682 and 1684 that gives the street its name.

The first political resident of the 'house at the back' was Oliver Cromwell who lived there from 1650–54, following the Civil War. For many years 10 Downing Street was the residence of the Chancellor of the Exchequer and only from 1902. when Arthur Balfour became Britain's leader, have Prime Ministers been expected to live at number 10.

Until 1779 number 10 was in fact number 5 of 15 houses in the street. Look carefully at the street view, as seen on television, and you will see that it has no handle, making it impossible to open from the outside.

The house next door

Adjacent to number 10 on the left is number 11, home of the Chancellor of the Exchequer. Within, numbers 10 and 11 are actually joined, so it is possible to walk easily from one to the other. Number 11 contains the large flat occupied by David Cameron and his family for six years from 2010. Chancellor George Osborne used it only as an office. Number 12, official residence of the Chief Whip, is in fact used as the Prime Minister's Press office. In 2018 Number 9 housed the department for exiting the European Union.

Fit for a president

Number 1600 Pennsylvania Avenue, Washington DC is the world famous address of the White House, official residence of the President of the United States. Following a contest to choose an architect, the cornerstone of the house designed by Irish born James Hoban was laid on 13 October 1792 and is named for the lime-based whitewash coating its sandstone walls.

Although George Washington oversaw the construction, carried out by both freed and enslaved African Americans and Europeans (including Scottish stonemasons), he never actually lived there. The first residents were John and Abigail Adams who moved in on

THE ONLY DEMISE The only premier to die at 10 Downing Street was Sir Henry Campbell Bannerman on 22 April 1908.

1 November 1800 followed by Thomas Jefferson who famously installed two water closets and in 1805 held the first 'open house' to the public. In 1814, during the tenancy of James Madison, British troops burned the house to the ground, only for it to be rebuilt in just three years under Hoban's direction.

Later additions to the house were the Oval Office, sited in an expanded executive wing in 1909, and Ellen Wilson's Rose Garden of 1913. The now famous West Wing was enlarged and a swimming pool added in the 1940s to enhance the daily life of polio victim Franklin D. Roosevelt. Today the six-floor house has 312 rooms, 35 bathrooms and 147 windows.

ON AND OFF THE RECORD

Number One London, or 149 Piccadilly got its nickname as the first house beyond the old tollgate at Hyde Park Corner. Built by architect Robert Adam from 1771–78 for the Lord Chancellor Lord Apsley, its most famous resident was the Duke of Wellington who bought it in 1817, two years after his victory at Waterloo, as a base for his newfound political career.

NUMBERS FOR THE POST

WHAT'S YOUR POSTCODE? TODAY THAT IS A QUESTION YOU'RE LIKELY TO BE ASKED ALMOST DAILY. POSTCODES, WHICH EVOLVED FROM THE DIVISION OF CITIES INTO NUMBERED DISTRICTS, ARE NOW AN INTEGRAL PART OF EVERYONE'S IDENTITY.

In 1840, Britain's Postmaster General Rowland Hill revolutionized the post by introducing the first postage stamp, the Penny Black. Sixteen years later, by which time 100 million of the country's annual items of posted mail were delivered in London, he devised the system of postal districts whose basis is still used today. The original area covered was a 12-mile (19-km) radius from the post office at St Martin's Le Grand near St Paul's Cathedral. Each district was assigned a compass point as a suffix followed by a number, although within a decade the NE district was dropped and S divided between SW and SE.

By 1917 further subdivisions were needed so numbers were added, each corresponding to the relevant sub post office. What remains confusing even today is that the numbers were not arranged cartographically but alphabetically. So while Hampstead is NW3, next door Golders Green is NW11. Cricklewood is NW2 and Hendon NW4. Similarly, SW15 is Putney and SW16 is far from adjacent Streatham. In 1932 districts defined by a number were approved for other cities such as Manchester, Birmingham and Liverpool.

It was the introduction of electromechanical letter sorting from the late 1950s that triggered the introduction of the postcodes that evolved into those of today. In 1959, Norwich was chosen as the first city for coding to be tested but only in 1974 was the whole of Britain post coded. Experiments with various formats were resolved so that today the postcode BA1 3BW indicates that an address is in the central area of Bath in which BA1, the outward code, indicates the city and 3BW, the inward code, the specific street.

Zipping along

In the United States, numbered postal zones were begun in large cities in 1943, as in Chicago 8, Illinois. The following year postal inspector Robert Moon suggested three-digit zip codes, but not until 1 July 1963 were optional five-number zip codes introduced nationally, by which time state names had been officially abbreviated and added as suffixes as in Illinois, IL 88467. Today, the ZIP+4 code is usual, the additional four digits identifying a specific site such as an apartment block or a recipient of high mail volumes.

UNIQUE COMBINATION In Canada letters and numbers are uniquely combined. BCV2V 3Z4 would represent an area in central Vancouver, British Columbia.

ROADS TO TAKE – NAVIGATING BY NUMBERS

FINDING OUR WAY FROM PLACE TO PLACE ON THE ROAD WOULD BE VIRTUALLY IMPOSSIBLE WITHOUT NUMBERING SYSTEMS. THESE VARY FROM COUNTRY TO COUNTRY BUT ALL SHARE THE COMMON GOAL OF ACCURATE ORIENTATION.

Britain's highway classification system was begun in theory in 1913 but not until 1923 did numbers begin to appear on the roads themselves and in road atlases. The system divided the country into zones radiating clockwise starting with London as a central hub, then moving north. The result was the following single-digit A roads we use today:

A1 – London to Edinburgh (the Great North Road)
A2 – London to Dover
A3 – London to Portsmouth
A4 – London to Avonmouth (the Great West Road)
A5 – London to Holyhead
A6 – Luton to Carlisle (but originally from Barnet in north London)
A7 – Edinburgh to Carlisle
A8 – Edinburgh to Greenock
A9 – Falkirk to Scrabaster (essentially John o'Groats)

From here, routes are numbered clockwise from the hub created by the single digit road. So London to Kings Lynn is the A10 and London to Norwich the A11 and so on. For less important roads additional numbers are added, so the road from Basingstoke to Exeter is the A303. The network of B roads works similarly, with most having 3 or 4 digit designations. And, like its A roads, Britain's motorways mirror the original system.

The notorious motorway

The M25, London's outer orbital notorious for its rush hour gridlock, was originally suggested by a Royal Commission in 1905 when MP Mr R W Perks recommended a circular road farther out (12 miles/21 km from Charing Cross) to be built to a width of 250 feet (76 m) and with a total length of 75 miles (121 km). These essentially became the north and south circular roads; the M25 was not begun until the 1970s. Today, at 117 miles (188 km), it is Europe's second longest city bypass. The final 13 miles (20 km) from Micklefield to South Mimms was opened – ahead of schedule – on 29 October 1986 by Prime Minister Margaret Thatcher. At least 150,000 vehicles make use of the motorway each day.

Travelling in Europe

In 1947, immediately after its foundation, the United Nations Economic Commission for Europe (UNECE) set to work to define a road numbering system for Europe. The result was the E system whose central tenet is that roads running north to south have odd numbers and those orientated east to west have even ones. Within these the lowest numbers are the most northerly and westerly. As a rule, E signs are green, with numerals in white.

Compared with the small distances of Britain's roads (which are included in some E schemes), E roads with numbers ending with 0 or 5 cover thousands of kilometers for example:

INTERSTATES EXTRAORDINARY

Longest east-west: I-90, Boston (Massachusetts) to Seattle (Washington) – 3,020 miles (4,861 km)

Longest north-south: I-95, Houlton (Maine) to Miami (Florida) 1,920 miles (3,090 km)

Highest elevation above sea level: I-70 in the Eisenhower Tunnel (Colorado)

E25 – Hook of Holland (Netherlands) to Palermo (Italy) – 1,830 km (1,137 miles)
E30 – Cork (Ireland) to Omsk (Russia) – 6,050 km (2,359 miles)
E35 – Amsterdam (Netherlands) to Rome (Italy) – 1,660 km (1,031 miles)
E55 – Helsingborg (Sweden) to Kalamata (Greece) – 2,920 km (1,814 miles)
E60 – Brest (France) to Irkeshtam (Kyrgyzstan) – 8,200 km (5,095 miles)

Perhaps more familiar to travellers in Europe are the so-called intermediate roads such as:

E03 – Cherbourg (France) to La Rochelle (France) – 470 km (292 miles)
E09 – Orléans (France) to Barcelona (Spain) – 967 km (601 miles)
E19 – Amsterdam (Netherlands) to Paris (France) – 520 km (323 miles)
E28 – Berlin (Germany) to Minsk (Belarus) – 1,230 km (764 miles)
E41 – Dortmund (Germany) to Altdorf (Switzerland) – 760 km (472 miles)
E49 – Magdeburg (Germany) to Karlovy Vary (Czech Republic) – 740 km (460 miles)
E52 – Strasbourg (Germany) to Salzburg (Switzerland) – 520 km (323 miles)
E62 – Nantes (France) to Genoa (Italy) – 1,290 km (801 miles)

66 – and other US routes

As in Europe, America's route numbering system allocates odd numbers to roads running north-south with numbers ending in 1 for major routes, and even numbers to those that are east-west, with major routes ending in 0. In north-south routes the lowest numbers are to the east, the territory first settled by immigrants, while on east-west roads the lowest numbers are to the north.

After 1903, when Horatio Nelson Jackson became the first person to drive from San Francisco to New York using dirt trails it was America's early auto trail associations who first came up with route designations. Wisconsin, in 1918, was the first state to number its highways. The Interstate Highway System has been in existence since 1956; highway numbers increase from west to east and south to north.

GET YOUR KICKS

Many mourned the demise of US 66 when it was taken out of the system in 1985. Also known as the Mother Road, America's Main Street or the Will Rogers Highway, it was first designated in November 1926 running originally the 2,448 miles (3,940 km) from Chicago to Santa Monica. Not only was it the way to 'go west young man' but became famous as a result of the enduring 1946 song (see Counting in song) that became a 1961 hit for Chuck Berry. The popular TV series of the same name ran from 1960 to 1964.

THE NUMBER TO CALL

WHEN HE MADE THE FIRST TELEPHONE CALL ON 10 MARCH 1876 SCOTSMAN AND INVENTOR ALEXANDER GRAHAM BELL COULD NEVER HAVE IMAGINED A WORLD OF MOBILE PHONES WITH TEN-DIGIT TELEPHONE NUMBERS THAT CAN BE USED AS MINI COMPUTERS.

Early phone calls were always directed to individuals at known addresses by local switchboards. The change to numbers came in the winter of 1879–80 during an outbreak of measles in Lowell Massachusetts where Dr Moses Greely Parker was so concerned that the town's four switchboard staff might fall ill that he suggested allocating numbers to the town's 200 subscribers to facilitate the speedy training of new operators.

As telephone ownership burgeoned and rotary dialling was introduced with 'holes' containing a number and up to 3 letters, more numbers were needed. In 1930, New York City was the first to adopt a 2-letter 5-number format such as BRooklyn 45685. In 1947 this system was standardized across the nation when AT&T created the North American Numbering Plan. With advances in technology, allowing direct dialling,

HELPFUL NETWORKS

Even if your mobile or cell phone is locked, or has no SIM card, and even if you are in a black spot with no signal, it is still possible in most parts of the world to make a 211, 911, 999 or any other emergency call, thanks to the way in which the network is configured to receive from any available network nearby. However this makes it extremely easy to dial an emergency number accidentally.

letters became changed to numbers, so that by the 1960s New York residents had numbers beginning 212; for those in Los Angeles they were 213 and in Chicago 312. Today a typical New York number might be 1-212-863-6600.

Across the Atlantic

Britain was quick to see the telephone's potential and by 1880 there were 248 subscribers to the Telephone Company. Numbers were gradually introduced and by 1914, some 1.5 million copies of the telephone book were printed. Among the numbers listed were Victoria 6913, the number for Buckingham Palace. But it took until 1927 for London to be the first city to introduce the standard of 3 letters indicating the local exchange followed by 4 digits, as in HOLborn 5547.

In 1968, subscriber trunk dialling (STD) finally allowed direct dialling

with an all-digit number independent of an exchange. With the exception of large cities, letters in the prefixes of old telephone numbers were translated into digits: 01 was for London, 021 for Birmingham, 031 for Edinburgh, 041 for Glasgow, 051 for Liverpool and 061 for Manchester. As the years have progressed prefixes have become longer. From 1990 addresses in inner London had the format 071-xxx-xxxx while outer London had the prefix 081. The change prompted disparaging remarks from residents of the city centre to those of the suburbs. Within five years these had been changed to 0171 and 0181.

With the introduction of mobile phones the UK needed yet more numbers and in 1997 began the start of 10-digit numbers with prefixes relating to the telephone provider. So Vodaphone, for example, which originally had numbers beginning 0370 now has numbers beginning 077.

MEMORABLE NUMBERS

• PEnnsylvania 65-0-0-0 was immortalized by the Glenn Miller Orchestra in 1940. The number belongs to the Hotel Pennsylvania, whose owner claims to have the oldest unchanged number in New York City.

• WHItehall 1212 was the number of London's Scotland Yard, headquarters of the Police Force. In many a movie thriller suspects were reported by dialling this number. Today the final digits of New Scotland Yard are still 1212.

• The world's most expensive number is 666-6666, a cell phone number auctioned in Qatar for charity in May 2006 reflecting the luckiness of six.

• For use in American movies the fictional exchange KLOndike was originally selected but was later changed to 555. The 'impossible' rule has been broken many times, as in *Fight Club* (1999), which used 288. In the UK it is 01632.

Emergency numbers

In the early days an emergency would simply mean contacting the telephone operator and reporting the problem. The world's first emergency number was the 999 still used today, first dialled in London in 1937 before being available countrywide. Dialling 999 triggered a flashing red light at the exchange to attract the operator's attention.

Settling a standard took much longer in North America. In 1946 Southern California began using 116 for emergencies. The design of the American phone switches made it impractical to use 999, and it was only on 16 February 1968 that Rankin Fite, Alabama Speaker of the House made the first 'official' 911 call. Initially Canada also used 999 but changed to match the USA in 1972.

In the European Union, 211 has been the accepted emergency number since 1972. France had a system of dialling 17 for the police and 18 for the fire brigade as early as 1913. Until the 1960s, Australia had no standard emergency number. Since then 000 has been the number to dial nationwide.

PIN – WHAT'S YOUR NUMBER?

ALTHOUGH WE CALL THEM PIN NUMBERS THIS TERM IS IN FACT A TAUTOLOGY, SINCE PIN STANDS FOR PERSONAL IDENTIFICATION NUMBER/S. AS WE ACCUMULATE EVER MORE OF THEM IT MAKES EXTRA SENSE TO KNOW HOW TO PICK THE MOST SECURE.

It was the arrival of ATMs (automatic teller machines) in 1967 to deliver cash in return for coded cheques after banking hours that led to the introduction of the PIN. Although patented by Scotsman and inventor James Goodfellow in 1965, the first cash card requiring a PIN was not issued until 1972, by Barclays Bank, for which the British inventor John Shepherd-Barron bears the credit. He had originally envisaged a 6-digit PIN, but revised the number after discovering that his wife could remember only 4 digits with ease. The 4-digit code is favoured worldwide, but Switzerland now demands 6 digits for increased security, and in many countries credit and debit cards are also issued with a 3-digit security code on the back which must be quoted for online transactions.

The safest PIN

For a 4-digit PIN there are 10,000 possible number combinations available, although it is still possible for competent hackers to crack 20 per cent of all PINs. Surprisingly, raising the number to 9 or 15 decreases the security because, for ease of remembering, more people use 123456789 or, particularly in the USA, their social security number. Despite the risk, more than 10 per cent of people use 1234 as their 4-digit PIN and 6 per cent settle for 1111. Other

0123 4567 8901 2345

8945. Or combine the numbers from two different dates.

Numbers can be useful in passwords too. Simply by changing a V to a 7 or an E to a 3 you can up the strength by more than 50 per cent. Or add numbers to the end of an unusual word for a similar effect.

popular combinations include 1212 (1.2 per cent), 7777 (0.75 per cent) and 4444 (0.5 per cent). Also common are 1984, 2001 and 0007 for would-be James Bonds. Thieves who can discover your birthdate will find it easy to crack a PIN based on it, but the most secure numbers are those supplied randomly by your bank or store, or those you can make up for yourself. A good trick is to think of a word (not your name) such as HIDE and convert the letters according to their place in the alphabet to give you

PHONE PROTECTION

Mobile phones, tablets and computers now have PIN protection as an obligation or option. If a PIN is entered incorrectly three times the SIM card will be blocked until you enter the unblocking code sent by your operator. Entering the wrong PIN ten times will result in permanent blocking.

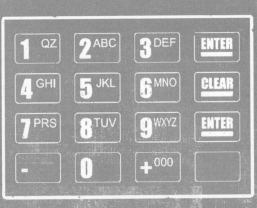

EDIBLE CONNECTIONS

FROM KETCHUP TO CHILLIES, AND FROM ICE CREAM TO ADDITIVES, NUMBERS HAVE SIGNIFICANCE IN THE FOODS THAT WE EAT FOR BOTH HEALTH AND ENJOYMENT.

Of all the numbers with foodie connections most famous are the Heinz '57 Varieties', now shorthand for anything with many parts, notably mongrel dogs. Henry J. Heinz, founder of the eponymous food company in Pittsburgh, USA, introduced the slogan in an advertising campaign of 1896. Even in 1892 the company was already selling more than 60 different products but Heinz chose 57 because 5 was his lucky number and 7 his wife's. And he

believed that 7 would have a positive 'psychological influence' over his prospective customers. It is said that hitting the '57' on the label of a ketchup bottle is the best spot to guarantee quick and easy pouring.

The 99 icecream – a filled cone with a Cadbury's flake inserted – is an enduringly favourite treat. The 99 Flake, a smaller version of the original developed in 1920 first appeared in 1930. The origin of the 99 prefix may come from the address of ice cream seller Stephen Arcari whose shop was at 99 Portobello High Street in Scotland. Or it could have been coined by an Italian ice cream seller in honour of the 'Boys of 99' – the last of the Italian conscripts of World War I who were born in 1899. Cadbury, however, suggest that it comes from the 99 men who traditionally formed the guard for the Italian monarch. A double 99 with two flakes added is often known as a 'bunny ears'.

Home cooking

Successful home cooking, but particularly baking, relies greatly on the accurate ingredient measuring. For example, the traditional Victoria sandwich sponge is made with 'the weight of two eggs' – which is approximately 125 g (4 oz). The cook striving for perfection would put the eggs on one side of a scale balance and measure, in turn, the flour, sugar and butter to exactly the same weight.

Most modern cookery books now express the weights and volumes of ingredients in metric measurement, so it is useful to know that 1 tablespoon = 15 ml and 1 teaspoon = 5 ml and to acquire a set of measuring spoons as well as accurate scales. The first cook

to emphasize the importance of careful measuring was the American Fannie Merritt Farmer (born in 1857) who recommended 'tin measuring-cups, divided into quarters or thirds, holding one half-pint, and tea and tablespoons of regular sizes.' Today's American cooks still measure by the cup, which has a volume of 240 ml (½ pint). To purists this has the disadvantage that ingredients vary in density, so a cup of flour (120 g about 4 oz) weighs twice as much as a cup of butter (240 g about 8 oz).

Hot numbers
That searing feeling of chilli pepper on the palate comes from the substance capsaicin. It is the capsaicin concentration that is used to calculate the heat of a chilli in Scoville heat units (SHUs), a numerical device invented by the American pharmacist Wilbur Scoville in 1912. On this scale the hottest pepper in the world is the Carolina Reaper rated at more than 2 million SHU. Not far behind come the Bhut jolokia or ghost pepper and the Spanish Naga chilli. In the mid range at around 100,000 units are the bird's eye chilli and the Scotch bonnet while the mildest include the Jalapeno (around 10,000) and the Pimento and Banana pepper at a mere 500.

Vitamin value
In an attempt to discover the cause of the fatal wasting disease beriberi, which appeared to be linked to a diet rich in polished rice, the Polish born American biochemist Casimir Funk discovered in 1912 that the rice husk contained a substance which he dubbed a 'vital amine' or vitamin as we know it today. Funk's vitamin B1, or thiamine, was the

first of the B vitamins, all of which are known by numbers.

When in 1920 another similar vitamin, found in dairy products and yeast extract was discovered it was named B2. This is riboflavin, essential for a healthy blood system. Other B vitamins, known with B1 and B2 and the 'B complex' are numbered 3 (niacin), 5 (pantothenic acid), 6 (pyridoxine), 7 (biotin), 9 (folic acid) and 12 (cobalamins). Together they protect from skin diseases, anaemia and heart failure, but because the body cannot store them they need to be consumed daily. The reason that some numbers are missing from the sequence comes from the fact that other substances were discovered and numbered but dropped because they were not 'true' vitamins.

Safely added
Look on the label of any processed food and you will see a list of E numbers. These are the codes given to all additives approved for safe use by the European Union and include many natural substances.

Some common E numbers include:
E102: Tartrazine – a yellow/orange colouring. May cause allergic reactions.

E150: Caramel – used to improve texture and add sweetness.

E162: Beetroot red – a natural red colouring.

E249–252: Nitrites and nitrates. Used to preserve meats and fish, including ham and bacon. Can cause allergic reactions and, in excess, are possibly carcinogenic.

E300–304: Ascorbic acid. A natural acid found in fruit used to prevent other foods such as apples turning brown. Known as an antioxidant.

E440: Pectins. Natural substances found in fruit such as plums used to set jams and jellies.

E621: Monosodium glutamate (MSG) – a flavour enhancer, found naturally in many savoury foods such as anchovies and tomatoes.

MORE THAN A MEAL Fast food restaurants have begun adding calorie counts to their meals but few if any would exceed the 4,556 calories estimated in the Mega Mel Burger served at Mel's Country Café in Texas which contains 1.5 pounds (680g) of ground beef, a pound of bacon, ¼ pound (13g) of American cheese, lettuce, tomatoes, pickle and bun.

COUNTING THE CALORIES

Whatever we eat, one good way of keeping track is by counting the calories it contains. One calorie is the energy needed to raise the temperature of 1 gram of water through 1°C (now usually defined as 4.1868 joules), which is a small amount, so the calories in food are usually expressed as kilocalories, one kilocalorie being the equivalent of 1,000 'small' calories.

Among the highest calorie foods are, per 100 gram (3½ ounce) serving:

Olive oil: 900 calories
Peanut butter: 589 calories
Milk chocolate: 535 calories
Coconut milk: 230 calories

And the lowest per 100 grams include (because they are largely composed of water):

Cucumber: 12 calories
Tomatoes: 16 calories
Broccoli: 28 calories
Grapefruit: 30 calories

SIZING UP OUR DRINKS

THE MEASURE OF WHAT WE DRINK, PARTICULARLY WHEN IT COMES TO ALCOHOL, RANGES FROM 'ONE FOR THE ROAD' TO MORE PRECISE CALCULATIONS OF THE ALCOHOL UNITS THAT MAY, IN EXCESS, ADVERSELY AFFECT OUR HEALTH.

Over indulgent drinking is the source of some colourful expressions. To be 'one over the eight', or slightly inebriated, refers to the eight pints of beer once regarded as a reasonable amount for a man to drink at the pub. Being a little worse for wear is to be 'half cut'. Before about 1800 the expression was to be 'half shaved', the inference being that a man was so drunk that he could not sit still for long enough for the barber to shave him and cut his hair. Even worse is to be 'three sheets in the wind', a phrase that comes from the sheet or rope joined to a sail which, if loose enough for the sail to flap, is said to be 'in the wind'.

How many units?

In 2016 the British government revised its guidelines for safe drinking, first issued in 1987, recommending that both men and women should regularly consume no more than 14 units of alcohol a week. This is a significant drop for men from the 1995 recommendations of 3–4 units a day for men and 2–3 for women.

Alcohol units are calculated by volume but also by the percentage of 'alcohol by volume' or ABV of each drink, and can be calculated to a good approximation using the equation:

ALCOHOL UNITS

Units = volume (ml) × ABV% ÷ 1,000

Or, more easily, make a note that these drinks comprise 14 units:
6 × 568 ml (1 pint) of 4% ABV beer
9 × 125 ml of 12% ABV champagne
6 × 175 ml 13% ABV wine
14 × 50 ml 20% ABV sherry or fortified wine
14 × 25 ml 40% ABV spirits

Size and name

The standard size of a bottle of wine is 75 ml or 0.75 litres but wine comes in other colourfully named bottle sizes, including:

Name	Volume (litres)
Piccolo, Pony or Split	0.1875
Jennie (champagne and many sweet wines such as Tokay)	0.5
Magnum	1.5
Jeraboam	3 or 4.5
Rehoboam	4.5
Methusela	6
Salamanzar	9
Balthazar or Belshazzar	12
Nebuchannezzar	15
Melchizdek or Midas (champagne)	30

Wine is traditionally stored in the cellars in bins, each given a number. Originally a bin number was a record of where maturing wine was stored in its cask, but today a bin number also refers to a wine's quality. Some bin numbers are prized by collectors: an Australian example is Penfolds Bin 389, a Cabernet/Shiraz blend.

Not so soft?

The popular soft drink 7 UP started life in the USA in 1929 with the far from snappy name of Bib-Label Lithiated Lemon-Lime Soda. It did indeed contain lithium citrate, a mood-stabilizing drug and, like Coca Cola, was marketed as a patent medicine. The inventor, Charles Leiper Grigg soon shortened the name to 7 Up Lithiated Lemon Soda but from 1936 it was being sold simply as 7 Up.

Grigg never revealed his reason for the name change, but the obvious conclusion is that, with sugar and carbonated water added, it was the number of basic ingredients. Or it might have been a reference to the atomic number of lithium, which is close to seven. The formula has been changed over the years but lithium remained an ingredient until 1950. Many variations are now on sale, including 7 Up Ten, containing just 10 calories, which was launched in 2013.

BY THREE

Triple sec, originally Curaçao triple sec, is named from the three times it is distilled in copper vats. First created in 1834 by Jean-Baptiste Combier in France's Loire Valley, this spirit is a mixture of peel from Haitian oranges, Normandy sugar beet, pure alcohol – and secret ingredients known only to the family.

OF YARNS, FABRICS AND CLOTHES

WHETHER CHOOSING A GARMENT FOR SIZE, OR FABRIC FOR ITS QUALITY, KNOWING THE CORRECT NUMBER CAN BE CRITICAL TO MAKING THE BEST PURCHASE.

With yarns, ply is the number of threads that are twisted together to make the finished thread and is applied particularly to knitting wools. For tights and stockings yarn weight is expressed, for example, as 7, 10 or 30 denier, a word derived from a low value French coin equal in weight to 1.2 g ($\frac{1}{24}$ oz).

For woven fabrics such as bed linen and towels, quality can be measured as a thread count, which is the number of threads per square inch. A 'standard' thread count would be around 150, a supreme quality one 200 or more. For silk, mommes measure the weight of a length of silk linen 45 in (114 cm) wide by 100 yards (91 m) long. Good silk bed linen will have a momme weight of over 16 and a thread count of 400 or higher. Raw silk weighs in at 35 to 40 mommes.

Fitted by numbers

The numbers used for indicating clothes sizes differ from country to country but actual sizing can vary according to the manufacturer and the brand. However these are useful guides:

Women's clothes

USA	0	2	4	6	8	10	12	14	16	18	20
UK	4	6	8	10	12	14	16	18	20	22	24
Australia	6	8	10	12	14	16	18	20	22	24	26
Germany, Scandinavia	30	32	34	36	38	40	42	44	46	48	50
France, Spain, Portugal	32	34	36	38	40	42	44	46	48	50	52
Italy	36	38	40	42	44	46	48	50	52	54	56

Men's suits and jackets

Australia, Europe	46	48	50	52	54	56	58	60	62
USA, UK	36	38	40	42	44	44	48	50	52

Men's shirts (by collar size)

USA/UK	14½	15	15½	16	16½	17	17½	18	18½
Australia/Europe	37	38	39	41	42	43	44	45	46

ALL IN THE NUMBER

• Technically denier is the mass in grams per 9,000 metres of fibre, and 1 denier is equal to 0.11mg per metre of thread.

• 'Double Two' shirts, each sold with easily detachable collars and, in addition, a complimentary replacement collar, a godsend before washing machines were widely affordable. They were first made in Wakefield, Yorkshire, in 1946 by Isaak Donner and Frank Myers' factory.

• Plus fours, a kind of men's knickerbocker, became particularly popular for sports in the 1920s. The 'four' refers to the 4 in (10cm) of additional cloth (often tweed) needed to extend the fabric below the knee. Plus twos are similar but with half the fabric required for a shorter result.

• A ten-gallon hat is the large, wide-brimmed hat traditionally worn by cowboys. The name refers to its supposed capacity.

ALL THAT GLITTERS

WHEN IT COMES TO THE PRECIOUS THINGS THAT WE LIKE TO WEAR, WHETHER GOLD, PLATINUM OR DIAMONDS, NUMBERS ARE ALL IMPORTANT IN ASSESSING PURITY, QUALITY AND VALUE.

The purity of gold is measured in karats. Pure gold, with its distinctive warm, bright yellow colour, is 24 karats, with no trace of other metals included. Most jewellery is made from 22 karat gold which contains 2 parts in 24 (8.3 per cent) of other metals such as silver, nickel and zinc, which makes it harder and more durable. More affordable and versatile yet is 18 karat gold – often stamped 750 or 0.75 to indicate that it is 75 per cent pure gold – which is similarly mixed with other metals. Rose gold is produced by adding copper, while white gold has metals such as silver and palladium incorporated.

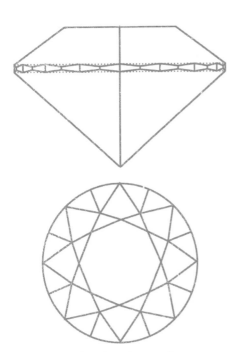

Round brilliant diamond cut

back to the viewer. For diamonds this is 2.417, which is high compared with other gems. For ruby, for example, it is only 1.7.

It is the cutting of a diamond that makes it special, allowing light to reflect from each of its sides or facets. The most common cut is the round brilliant which has 57 facets. Of these 33 are on the crown or top, above the so-called girdle and 25 on the lower part or pavilion which tapers to a point. The girdle itself may also have 32, 64, 80 or 96 minute facets. It was the Polish diamond cutter and engineer Marcel Tolkowsky who 'invented' this modern diamond cut which optimizes the diamond's properties; his influential book *Diamond Design* was published in 1919.

The largest uncut quality diamond ever found weighed 3106.75 carats (621.35 g) and was cut into 105 individual diamonds. Largest of these were the Cullinan I or the Great Star of Africa at 530.2 carats (106.04 g), and the Cullinan II or Lesser Star of Africa, weighing 317.4 carats (63.48 g). Both now form part of Britain's Crown Jewels.

Platinum, increasingly popular for jewellery, is also graded by purity. Best quality platinum is graded 950, meaning that 5 per cent of it is composed of another metal, usually ruthenium, copper, cobalt, iridium, rhodium or palladium. Lower grades are marked 900, 850 and 585. As with gold, the pure metal is soft, so the alloys are often preferable for durability.

Sheer brilliance

Like gold, the diamonds are weighed in carats. One carat weighs ⅕ gram and is divided into 100 points. But the finished quality of a diamond depends on how it disperses light. Key to this are its refractive index (RI), which measures the amount of light that is reflected

FROM THE EAST

Of all the world's diamonds 11 out of 12 are processed in India where some 1.3 million people are employed in the business. Diamonds account for 14 per cent of India's annual exports.

BEAUTY BY NUMBERS

SOME OF THE WORLD'S MOST ICONIC FRAGRANCES ARE KNOWN AS MUCH BY THEIR NUMBER AS THEIR NAME AND ALL HAVE FASCINATING HISTORIES. A TRAINED PERFUMIER WILL BE ABLE TO COMMIT SOME 3,000 SCENTS TO MEMORY.

The oldest 'numbered' fragrance, 4711 Eau de Cologne, dates to the 18th century when Johann Maria Farina moved from Italy to Cologne and began to make and sell a fragrance containing citrus oils, rosemary and lavender. Legend has it that in 1792 a young man named Wilhelm Mülhens received the recipe for an *aqua mirabilis* (intended for both external and internal use) as a wedding gift from a Carthusian monk.

In 1803 the enterprising Mülhens somewhat deviously obtained the rights to the Farina name. After a series of lawsuits he eventually adopted the name '4711' for his company, based on the number given to the small factory in a street called Glockengasse, in which Mülhens was listed as a tenant. The numbering of buildings had been carried out by law after French troops occupied the city in 1794.

The Chanel story

The French couturier 'Coco' (Gabrielle) Chanel believed five to be a special number. For the girl brought up from the age of 12 in a Cistercian orphanage it symbolized the essence of mysticism and spiritualism. On her daily path to prayer she walked along circular paths laid out in patterns that repeated the number five. So when, in 1920, she was presented with samples of her new perfume numbered 1 to 5 and 20 to 24 she chose her enduringly famous No.5 which, in its day, epitomized the

SENSUAL NUMBERS 212 Sexy and 212 VIP are two of the fragrances developed in the late 1990s for a new generation by Carolina Herrera, daughter of the Venezuelan-American dress designer of the same name. The number 212 refers to the New York dialling code, the place with pure 'buzz' for the young.

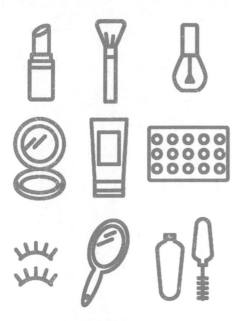

liberated energy of 1920s women. '... we will let this sample number five keep the name it has already' she said, 'it will bring good luck'.

In 1922, a year after the launch of No.5, the fresher, more floral Chanel No.22 made its debut. No.19, with its woody-green scent, came much later in 1971, the year before her death. It was named to commemorate Coco's birthday on 19 August.

Brand by number

On the high street Boots No7 is among the best-known and trusted cosmetic brands. Founded in 1849 by Jesse Boot to produce drugs, the company was sold to the American Drug Company in 1920 only to be bought back in 1933 by John Boot, Jesse's son. John then decided to launch his own brand and the first No7 lines – 11 skincare products – were first sold in 1935. No7 hit the headlines in 2007 when it launched its Protect and Perfect anti-ageing serum, which proved so popular and effective in smoothing skin that stores even had to draw up waiting lists. Boots No17 brand for teenagers reached the shops in 1968.

FOR OUR LEISURE
AND ENTERTAINMENT

'One, two, buckle my shoe ...' begins one of the oldest of many nursery rhymes long proved successful in teaching young children to count and to appreciate numbers. And from an early age we have all had common sense instilled into us with such proverbs as 'Two's company, three's a crowd' and 'There are only 24 hours in a day'. More complex than these are the numbers that define the poetry we so enjoy, from the standard 14 lines of the sonnet and five of the limerick to the number rules that govern the metres and feet of verse. Music, too, is essentially mathematical as is, on a less elevated level, the popular game of bingo.

Numbers feature consistently in the titles of the books, films and songs that we relish, for a diversity of reasons. *Catch-22*, *The Thirty-Nine Steps* and *The Seven Pillars of Wisdom*; *BUtterfield 8*, *21 Grams* and *Five Easy Pieces*; '50 Ways to Leave Your Lover', '5-4-3-2-1' and '99 Red Balloons' are among those that have the most memorable back stories.

Sports lovers are ever keen to show off their knowledge and impress with statistics of many kinds, from record football transfer fees to record rounds in golf and cricketers' top scores. While it is impossible to be comprehensive here, almost all the most popular sports are included, along with those such as darts and snooker which depend intrinsically on numbers. Finally, you can discover how to calculate the odds of winning the lottery, see how dice games work and discover how such daily mental workouts as Sudoku came into our lives.

PROVERBS AND SAYINGS

'WISE MEN' IT IS SAID, 'MAKE PROVERBS AND FOOLS REPEAT THEM.' THIS MAY BE SO, BUT PROVERBS AND SAYINGS HAVE LONG HELPED PEOPLE TO COMMENT ON THEIR DAILY LIVES, AND PASS THEIR EXPERIENCE TO FUTURE GENERATIONS. MANY OF THESE SAWS USE NUMBERS TO MAKE THEIR POINT.

The notion that cooperation is admirable and effective is expressed in many proverbs in which 'one' is used as a synonym for the common good as in 'All for one and one for all' and 'One enemy is too many and a hundred friends too few'. By contrast, to be alone is a disadvantage, as in 'Two heads are better than one' and 'It takes two to tango'. And even when bad luck does come your way it is comforting to think that you might be 'Third time lucky' or even be able to have 'Two bites at the cherry'.

Being realistic

Many proverbs are intended to bring us down to earth. We are reminded that 'Two blacks don't make a white', that 'There are only 24 hours in the day' and that 'You can't be in two places at once'. We are urged to have patience and take life 'One day at a time' and, if we make mistakes, reminded that 'A hundred pounds of sorrow pays not one ounce of debt'. However we can make the most of what we have by remembering that 'One foot is better than two crutches'.

If we are over optimistic, then the truth that 'One swallow doesn't make a summer' will remind us of reality. Equally it is good to know that an argument can be 'Six of one and half a dozen of the other' and

that 'Six feet of earth (that is, the grave) make all men equal'. If confused we use numbers to express that we are 'At sixes and sevens', but we can always 'Put two and two together'.

Seven and nine

It is no coincidence that the lucky number seven expresses the height of pleasure when we are in 'seventh heaven'. For the gardener, seven is the number to remember when it comes to removing weeds for if allowed to mature the saying 'One years' seed, seven years' weed' may come true. Like cats we might desire their 'nine lives', and of course the frugal housewife knows that 'A stitch in time saves nine'.

ADDED HUMOUR

Parodying the proverb 'When one door shuts another one opens' the comedian Spike Milligan professed that it should end '... another one closes'.

BINGO LINGO

THE EVER-POPULAR GAME OF BINGO OR HOUSEY-HOUSEY, WITH ITS OWN NUMERICAL LANGUAGE, HAS A SURPRISINGLY LONG HISTORY.

Bingo began life in Italy where, following the country's unification in 1530, it was played as a lottery to raise government funds. Much later it was adopted and enjoyed by the French aristocracy and in the 1800s played in Germany to encourage children to learn their numbers. The game's popularity in Britain stems from World War I when soldiers played it to pass the time, and divert their minds, in the trenches.

The full house

The idea of bingo is to be the first to get 'full house' by filling a card containing a selection of numbers between 1 and 90 (in the US 1 to 75) by matching them with those drawn by a caller. Originally known as 'beano', because beans were used as card markers, the name change was engineered by toy salesman Edwin S. Lowe, after he heard an American competitor accidentally shout 'bingo'.

Lowe then hired maths professor Carl Leffler to help him work out how to maximize the number combinations on the cards. The original bingo card consisted of 3 horizontal and 9 vertical rows of squares with 4 randomly placed blanks in each horizontal row and the remaining squares filled with a selection of numbers, with no repeats.

Number nicknames

Over the years, bingo numbers have acquired humorous, often slightly risqué nicknames based on everything from simple rhyme to military connections reflecting the game's years of evolution.

Kelly's Eye – number one – has no decisive origin. It may come from the Australian outlaw Ned Kelly, from the musical hall song 'Has Anyone Here Seen Kelly', or a comic strip in which Kelly owned a magic amulet.

The good bingo caller will shout them with relish. These are some of the best examples:

Lookalikes simply reflect the shape of the number:
2 – one little duck; 22 – two little ducks; 11 – legs eleven; 7 – one crutch; 77 – two crutches; 27 – duck and crutch; 8 – one fat lady; 81 – fat lady with a walking stick; 88 – two fat ladies.

Rhymes are self explanatory:
2 – me and you; 3 – cup of tea; 4 and 24 – knock at the door; 5 – man alive; 8 – garden gate; 15 – young and keen; 25 – duck and dive; 28 – in a state; 29 – rise and shine; 30 – Burlington Bertie (from the music hall song) or dirty Gertie (from a London statue erected in 1927 and a bawdy World

War II song); 31 – get up and run; 32 – buckle my shoe; 33 – all the threes (fish, chips and peas); 34 – ask for more; 52 and 72 – Danny La Rue or chicken vindaloo; 54 – man at the door; 55 – musty hive; 59 – the Brighton Line (first 2 numbers of the original telephone exchange); 60 – butler's getting frisky; 62 – tickety boo (meaning feeling well); 66 – clickety click; 71 – bang on the drum; 73 – queen bee or under the tree; 85 – staying alive; 86 – between the sticks (the goalkeeper); 87 – Torquay in Devon.

All in the numbers reflect the way numbers add up, their names and associations with fortune:
7 – lucky; 12 – one dozen; 13 – unlucky for some; 20 – one score; 36 – three dozen; 45 – half way there (to 90); 48 –

four dozen; 89 – almost there; 90 – top of the shop (the largest number).

Social and everyday connections, often outdated, still find their way to the bingo hall:
10 – Prime Minister's den (in Downing Street); 14 – the lawnmower (number of blades on the original machine); 16 – never been kissed (the age of consent in the UK); 18 – coming of age; 21 – key of the door (traditional age of majority) or royal salute (guns); 26 – half a crown (2s 6d in 'old' money); 57 – Heinz varieties; 64 – almost retired (the long-time male retirement age); 65 – stop work; 72 – par for the course (as in golf).

Music, television, books and films connect with some numbers:
17 – Dancing Queen (from the Abba song) 23 – the Lord's my Shepherd (from the psalm); 39 – steps (from the novel); 42 – a street in Manhattan; 49 – PC (from the 50s radio show 'PC 49'); 50 – Hawaii Five-O; 64 – The Beatles' number; 76 – trombones (from *The Music Man*); 77 – Sunset Strip (the TV series).

Military connections still linger in bingo lingo:
9 – doctor's orders, the number of the laxative pill given to troops in World War II; 22 – a concert party.

BOOKS WITH NUMBERS

A NUMBER IN THE TITLE OF A BOOK OFTEN GIVES THE READER AN IMMEDIATE IDEA OF THE CONTENT WITHIN, BUT IT CAN BE MORE SUBTLE. SOME 'NUMBERED' TITLES, SUCH AS *CATCH-22*, HAVE EVEN BECOME EMBEDDED INTO THE LANGUAGE AND MANY HAVE BEEN MADE INTO SUCCESSFUL FILMS OR TELEVISION SERIES.

Adventure and Crime

Jules Verne, French master of adventure, invented Phileas Fogg who, for a wager of £20,000 (more than £2 million today) was the hero of *Around the World in 80 Days* (1873). Accompanied by his French valet Jean Passpartout he encounters dangers and delays at every stage. Seemingly five minutes late to win his bet he is 'saved' by having crossed the international date line (see Lines on the map).

In 1844, Alexandre Dumas' *The Three Musketeers* began publication in serial form. Set in the 17th century the trio – Athos, Porthos and Aramis – are befriended by the young nobleman D'Artagnan. It is a story of politics, personal rivalry and romance complete with much duelling! Also initially serialized from 1915, John Buchan's *The Thirty-Nine Steps* was the first to feature his action hero Richard Hannay. Set in 1914, shortly before the outbreak of war, it is a spy story in which keeping secrets from the enemy is crucial. The 39 steps on the Kent coast feature in the final dénoument, where the enemy landing is thwarted.

In Arthur Conan Doyle's second Sherlock Holmes novel of 1890, *The Sign of Four* (originally *The Sign of the Four*) includes the famous saying: 'How often have I said to you that when you have eliminated the impossible, whatever remains, *however improbable*, must be the truth?' The book's complex plot involves the Indian Rebellion of 1857, a lost father and the receipt of a mysterious set of pearls. The 'Sign of Four' is a note left on the dead father's body relating to a secret pact between four convicts.

Agatha Christie's Miss Marple first appeared in *The Thirteen Problems*, a short story collection published in 1927. Her other famous detective, Hercule Poirot features in *Five Little Pigs* (1943) in which the daughter of an artist whose beautiful mother is wrongly executed for murder 14 years previously. The five are the suspects, each possessing characteristics of the nursery rhyme 'little piggies' who 'went to market, stayed at home, ate roast beef, had none and cried "wee wee wee" all the way home'.

In *The Five Red Herrings* (1931), Dorothy L. Sayers sets a puzzle for her readers which is eventually solved by detective Lord Peter Wimsey. Set in Galway, Scotland it involves the death of a drunken artist and an unfinished painting. The red herrings are the false leads discarded before the culprit, the sixth of the set, is finally revealed. Different indeed is Alexander McCall Smith's series of novels begun in 1998. Set in Botswana, star of *The No1 Ladies' Detective Agency* is chief investigator Mma Precious Ramotswe, the country's first female detective, whose success lies in her skill in discovering her suspects' true characters.

Tales from history

Paris and London before and during the French Revolution are the settings in Charles Dickens' *A Tale of Two Cities* (1859) which begins with the famous phrase: 'It was the best of times, it was the worst of times ....' The story revolves around a Dr Manette and his daughter Lucie, and the émigré Charles Darnay. At the book's conclusion Darnay is spared the guillotine by Sydney Carton who takes his place.

Between 1916 and 1918, 'Lawrence of Arabia' – Captain TE Lawrence – served in the British army as a liaison officer amongst rebel forces when the Arabs revolted against the rule of the Ottoman Turks. Lawrence's experiences, based on his extensive notes, are recorded in *The Seven Pillars of Wisdom*, first published in 1926. The book includes such incidents as the blowing up of train lines and the offensive to liberate Damascus. The book's title is drawn from both the Seven Pillars of the House of Wisdom

from the Old Testament Book of Proverbs and a poem by Robert Graves, which is quoted in the book's dedication to 'S.A'. The poem's first verse runs:

> I loved you, so I drew these tides of
> Men into my hands
> And wrote my will across the
> Sky in stars
> To earn you freedom, the seven
> Pillared worthy house,
> That your eyes might be
> Shining for me
> When I came

Lawrence never revealed the identity of S.A. but many think that it is the Arab boy Selim Ahmed of whom he was most fond.

In *Seven Years in Tibet: My Life Before, During and After* (1952) the Austrian mountaineer Heinrich Harrer recounts his life between 1944 and 1951, his escape from a British internment camp in India and how he became a friend and tutor to the 14th Dalai Lama at the time of China's takeover of Tibet in 1950. World War II is also the setting for *Catch-22* (1961), Joseph Heller's novel in which a group of airmen flying missions over Italy are paradoxically declared mentally unfit to fly but could not actually be excused from doing so. The title has become shorthand for an insoluble puzzle. Despite its graphic descriptions of warfare, the books ends with an upbeat escape story.

Alexander Solzhenitsyn's *One Day in*

CATCH-22

Twenty Thousand Leagues Under the Sea

the Life of Ivan Denisovich, is an intimate story of 1950s Stalinist repression, and caused a storm when published in 1960. In this brutally shocking history of life in a labour camp as experienced over 24 hours, we read of forced labour in temperatures of -40 degrees centigrade, of limited food and bedding – and how solidarity between the inmates helps them to survive.

In the modern mother-daughter tale *A Thousand Splendid Suns* (2007) by the Afghan-American Khaled Hosseni the lives of Mariam and Laila become intertwined in late 20th century Kabul. It is a revelation of women's existence under Taliban rule, an adventure and a love story. The title, describing the beauty of Afghanistan, comes from a 17th-century Persian poem.

Science fiction

The mysteries of the deep fascinated Jules Verne and his *Twenty Thousand Leagues Under the Sea* (1870) recounts the serial sightings of a mysterious sea monster. When found and attacked the creature destroys the adventurers' ship and they make the beast, Nautilus (in fact a submarine commanded by Captain Nemo), their home. Now follows a series of amazing undersea discoveries and life-threatening attacks. Remarkably, the book forecasts much of modern undersea exploration.

In 1949 English author George Orwell published his dystopian *Nineteen Eighty-four*. In what was once Great Britain, its characters live in Airstrip One, a province of Oceania. War,

FARENHEIT 451

Guy Montag, an official censor, after seeing a woman burnt alive rather than give up her books, joins a resistance group dedicated to reading and memorizing the world's most important works.

oppression and government surveillance are constant; individualism is banned 'thoughtcrime' a routine charge. Overseeing the tyranny is Big Brother, while the role of Winston Smith is to rewrite historical records. Today, 'Big Brother' and 'Room 101' are television series and 1984 remains a catchphrase for state oppression.

Based on his own World War II experiences, Kurt Vonnegut's disturbing satire *Slaughterhouse-Five*, subtitled *The Children's Crusade: A Duty-Dance with Death* (1969) centres on how Billy Pilgrim survives the bombing of Dresden and imprisonment in *Sachlachthof-fünf*. Pilgrim believes that he was in fact held captive in an alien zoo and experienced time travel back to the events of his past.

American author Ray Bradbury chose *Fahrenheit 451* for his dystopian 1953 novel because at this temperature the paper of a book will catch fire and burn. Inspired by his concerns for freedom in the McCarthy era, he imagines a future society in which books are both banned and set alight by 'firemen'. The hero

For readers' amusement
Originally intended as a travel guide, Jerome K. Jerome's 1889 *Three Men in a Boat (To Say Nothing of the Dog)* recounts a two-week boat trip from Kingston upon Thames to Oxford and back. Accompanying him are George and Harris, (based on his real-life friends, George Wingrave and Carl Hentschel), and the fictional dog Montmorency. Hilarious descriptions include Uncle Podger, and his attempt to hang pictures, to cooking an 'Irish stew' complete with water rat. The 1900 sequel, *Three Men on the Bummel* takes the trio on a cycling trip through the Black Forest.

Constantly in print since 1930, the title of W.C. Sellar and R.J. Yeatman's book reveals all: *1066 and All That: A Memorable History of England, comprising all the parts you can remember, including 103 Good Things, 5 Bad Kings and 2 Genuine Dates*. Facts are humorously warped and there is word play galore, ranging from the Venomous Bede to the Disillusion of the Monasteries and the Industrial Revelation – and even some joke test papers for readers to attempt.

Sue Townsend's Adrian Albert Mole made his debut in a BBC radio play in

1982 and in the same year appeared in print in *The Secret Diary of Adrian Mole, Aged 13¾*. The first in the eight-volume series probes Adrian's inner desires, from marrying his teenage sweetheart Pandora, to publishing his poetry and fiction to becoming financially secure. He also wants to be good, opening on 1 January 1981 with: 'I will help the blind across the road'. The book is set against the backdrop of his parents' divorce and the politics of 1980s Britain under Margaret Thatcher.

As Swedish author Jonas Jonasson's 2009 comic novel *The Hundred-Year-Old-Man Who Climbed Out of the Window and Disappeared* (2009) opens, Allan Karlsson is anticipating his retirement home birthday party. Rather than celebrate he climbs out of the window in his slippers and makes for the bus stop. In the ensuing story, which involves accidental meetings with drug dealers, his life is told in fantastical flashbacks ranging from helping to make the atom bomb to plotting the assassination of Winston Churchill.

Myth, legend and fantasy

One Thousand and One Nights, also known as *The Arabian Nights*, is a collection of never-ending folk tales from many authors and incorporates material from Arab, Persian, Turkish, Greek, and Indian sources, probably dating from the 8th century onwards. Even until the 18th century, European translators were adding new tales such as 'Aladdin and His Lamp' to the original collection, which included such classics as 'The Seven Voyages of Sinbad the Sailor' and 'The Three Apples'.

The tales are told by Scheherazade, a virgin vizier's daughter condemned to execution on the night of her forced marriage to king Shahryar, whose aim was to marry a virgin each day – and execute each in turn. However he is so enthralled by her unfinished tales of history, love, tragedy, humour and erotica that the telling continues for 1,001 nights (probably shorthand for a large number), before he falls in love with her and spares her life.

Ghosts symbolizing the past haunt the pages of *One Hundred Years of Solitude* (1967) by the magical realist Colombian Gabriel García Márquez. It is the story of the Buendía family and the town of Macondo invented by the patriarch José Arcadio, which is initially isolated. As generations proceed, the town becomes opened to the outside world and its realities, including civil war, massacre and the influence of technology. In a tragic end the town is destroyed by a hurricane.

The tale of 'The Three Apples' is told in *The Arabian Nights*

By mid 2015 some 125 million copies of *Fifty Shades of Grey* had been sold worldwide and it had been translated into 52 languages. Less successful were the follow up titles *Fifty Shades Darker* and *Fifty Shades Freed* (both 2012).

Expressions of love and friendship
In 1949 the New York author Helene Hanff was searching in vain for some obscure classics when she spotted an advertisement in the British weekly *The Saturday Review*. Then followed a 20-year correspondence between Hanff and Frank Doel, chief buyer of the antiquarian booksellers Marks&Co, and a lasting friendship with Doel and his staff. *84 Charing Cross Road*, the shop's location, became the title of Hanff's 1970 book, which also recounts such actions as sending food parcels to a Britain still undergoing food rationing.

Starting on St Swithin's Day, 15 July 1988, each chapter of David Nicholls 2009 novel *One Day*, consistently a year apart, follows Dexter and Emma from their first night together following graduation from Edinburgh University. They then go their separate ways in life and love but remain friends. An attempt to resume their relationship ends in another parting; when they finally marry their joy is short lived.

Self-publishing reached a new zenith in 2011 when E.L. James' erotic novel *Fifty Shades of Grey* was first made available online and print on demand. When released by Vintage books that year it became an instant best seller. The story revolves around the sexual relationship between student Anastasia 'Ana' Steele and wealthy Seattle entrepreneur Christian Grey and explores, often in graphic detail, such topics as sexual dominance and submission.

Children's books
The original 19th-century fairy tale of *Goldilocks and the Three Bears* was a scary encounter that has become softened with time. In the original the female intruder, having eaten the bears' porridge and slept in their beds, jumps from the window on the bears' return, never to be seen again.

From the pen of Enid Blyton came both the *Famous Five* and *Secret Seven* series in which children face dangers and solve crimes. Most famous are the 'five' characters – Dick, George, Anne, George (Georgina) and Timmy the dog. *Five on a Treasure Island*, published in

Goldilocks and the Three Bears

1942 was the first of 21 best-selling adventures. In recent years the five have become the subject of spoofs such as *Five On Brexit Island* (2016).

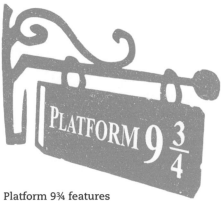

PLATFORM 9¾

Platform 9¾ features in the Harry Potter series

YOUNG PEOPLE'S FAVOURITES

Not the title of a book but famous nonetheless is Platform 9¾ at London's Kings Cross Station. This is the departure point for the Hogwarts Express boarded by Harry Potter and his fellow students in JK Rowling's super-selling series.

Among Beatrix Potter's enduring animal stories is *The Tale of Two Bad Mice* who create havoc in a doll's house.

THE LIBRARY BY NUMBERS

In 1876 the American librarian Melvil Dewey published the original version of his book classification index which, in essence, is still used today to make library books in different subject areas easy to find. Now known as the Dewey decimal system, major subjects are classified like this:

000 – Computer science, information and general works
100 – Philosophy and psychology
200 – Religion
300 – Social sciences
400 – Language
500 – Pure Science
600 – Technology
700 – Arts and recreation
800 – Literature
900 – History and geography

Each is then broken down further, so that within the arts for example Painting and paintings, category 750, is composed of the divisions: 751 Techniques, procedures, apparatus, equipment, materials, forms; 752 Colour; 753 Symbolism, allegory, mythology, legend; 754 Genre paintings; 755 Religion; 757 Human figures; 758 Nature, architectural subjects and cityscapes, other specific subjects; 759 History, geographic treatment, biography. Category 756 is not currently in use.

IN THE FILM TITLE

THE REASONS FOR INCLUDING NUMBERS IN FILM TITLES ARE OFTEN OBVIOUS BUT SOMETIMES SURPRISING. THESE ARE SOME INTERNATIONAL AND PERSONAL FAVOURITES, MANY OF THEM OSCAR WINNERS AND NOMINEES.

One Flew Over the Cuckoo's Nest (1975)
Finding himself transferred to a mental institution from a prison farm, after pleading insanity, the rebellious Randle Patrick McMurphy enters a battle of wits with the oppressive regime led by Nurse Ratched. Before long all the patients are affected and band together to express their disapproval with deadly results.

CHOOSING A TITLE
The title of *One Flew Over the Cuckoo's Nest* comes from a children's rhyme about three geese, which also serves as the epigraph: 'One flew east, one flew west,/One flew over the cuckoo's nest'.

The Taking of Pelham One Two Three (1974)
At successive New York subway stations four seemingly unconnected men board the train Pelham1:23 and take over its control, demanding $1 million ransom for 18 hostages. The ransom is paid, but now the hijackers have to contend with the ensuing police led by veteran Lt. Zach Garber.

Three Billboards outside Ebbing, Missouri (2018)
Angered by lack of progress made by local police in finding perpetrators of her daughter's brutal murder, a mother installs three controversial billboards on the outskirts of town to goad the authorities into action. Her decision leads to a clash with both the chief of police and his second-in-command who also has anger issues.

Three Colors Blue (1993)
After surviving a road accident in which her composer husband and young daughter meet tragic deaths, the grieving Julie tries to hide from the world. But in busy Paris she meets an old friend, Olivier who, having long loved her, brings her back to life's realities. The French trilogy was completed with *Three Colors Red* (1994) in which the death of a pet dog leads to a strange liaison between a part-time model and a judge, and *Three Colors White* (1994) featuring a Polish divorcee and hairdresser who takes revenge on his ex wife after being smuggled back to Warsaw but is thwarted when love intervenes.

Three Kings (1999)
In this satirical action movie set in the immediate aftermath of the Gulf War (fought from 2 August 1990 to 28 February 1991), four US soldiers set out to steal a hoard of gold taken from Kuwait by Saddam Hussein. Three (the 'kings') are rescued by rebels, but the fourth is captured and tortured by Iraqi intelligence. In return for his release the three agree to assist in fighting Saddam's Elite Guard.

Three Men and a Baby **(1987)**
An American comedy based on the 1985
French film *Trois hommes et un couffin*
(*Three Men and a Cradle*) in which three
bachelors struggle to raise Mary, the love
child of one of them, after she is left on
their doorstep. Accidents, drug dealing
and joint fatherhood create a bond that
is jeopardized when Mary's mother
Sylvia comes to claim her. In the 1990
sequel, *Three Men and a Little Lady* the
trio are devastated when Sylvia decides
to take Mary to England with her new
fiancé. The three follow in pursuit of the
happy ending.

Four Weddings and a Funeral **(1994)**
Charles, the archetypal Englishman
and his 'set' attend many weddings, but
true love is hard to find. When Charles
meets the beautiful American Carrie at
a wedding he thinks she is 'the one' but
she remains remote and unavailable.
They continue to meet at weddings and
the film's memorable funeral before
finally realizing that their destiny is
together.

Five Easy Pieces **(1970)**
Once a child piano prodigy from a well-
to-do family, American oil-rig worker
Bobby Dupea returns to his father's
death bed with his pregnant waitress
girlfriend Rayette, but abandons her in a
motel before reaching the family home.
She goes after him, but by now Bobby is
attracted to Catherine, the young pianist
engaged to Bobby's brother. The title
mirrors the five classical piano pieces
that dominate the score.

Six Degrees of Separation **(1993)**
Based on a true story, this US drama
mystery accepts the premise that we are

all separated from anyone in the world
by just six steps. Con artist Paul appears
one night at the door of art dealer Flan
Kittredge and his wife Ouisa claiming to
be a college friend of the couple's two
children. Taken in by his charm they are
shocked when he brings home a hustler
and his past schemes are revealed.

The Sixth Sense **(1999)**
In this mystery thriller, young Cole
Sear is regularly visited by ghosts,
which present him with a series of
unsolved and troubling issues. Only
his psychologist Dr Malcolm Crowe is
allowed to share the secret of Cole's
supernatural powers. The outcome is a
surprise for them both.

Seven Samurai (1954)
In this Japanese classic, set in 1586, the inhabitants of a farming village hire the services of seven *ronin* (samurai without masters) to combat the bandits who they know will come and steal their crops. When the bandits do appear, battle ensues with both villagers and samurai. Although the bandit chief is finally slain, only three samurai survive.

The Magnificent Seven (1960)
An American adaptation of *Seven Samurai* set in the Old West in which a group of US gunfighters are hired by Mexican border villagers to protect them from marauders intent on stealing their food. Following a shootout the villagers escort them away but they return to finish the job in which only three survive but the bandits depart for good.

Se7en (1995)
Set in a city beset with serial killings, police detective William Somerset embarks on his final case in partnership with short-tempered colleague David Mills. What emerges is that the life story of each victim is related to one of the seven deadly sins. In the final scene 'wrath' the killer meets his end.

Seven Brides for Seven Brothers (1954)
In this romantic musical, newly-wed Milly is shocked when she meets her husband Adam's six ill-mannered brothers with whom she now has to share a home. Undaunted she takes them in hand, but her efforts backfire when they kidnap six local girls during a barn-raising celebration. Finally, despite the villagers' attempts to avenge the kidnappings, all six couples wed.

The Seven Year Itch (1955)
While his wife is on vacation a New York publisher discovers that a beautiful model has moved in next door. Having fallen for her, he embarks on a series of daydreams, imagining what life would have been like had he been unfaithful to his wife. He eventually comes to his senses and leaves the city to join his family.

BUtterfield 8 (1960)
In this intense drama Gloria Wandrous, a New York call girl, mistakenly believes that her lover, married man Weston Liggett, will leave his wife for her. Liggett does finally decide to choose Gloria but the movie ends in tragedy when she is killed in a car crash. The title, with its distinctive use of capitals, comes from the call service serving Manhattan's Upper East Side (see The number to call).

8½ (Otto e mezzo) (1963)

Titled from the director Federico Fellini's own eight and a half experiences in movie directing, this semi-biographical Italian comedy-drama charts the ups and downs of Guido Anselmi, a frustrated film director attempting to complete a science fiction epic but suffering from creative block.

9 to 5 (1980)

The hours of the working day lend the title to this US comedy with its memorable theme song in which three working women dream of getting the better of their boss who is not only an autocratic egotist but sexist, untruthful and bigoted. In the end they get their just rewards.

10 Rillington Place (1971)

The film's title is the address of serial killer John Christie where, posing as a qualified doctor, he murders women including Beryl, the wife of his mentally challenged lodger Timothy Evans, and their baby Geraldine. Christie succeeds in pinning the blame on innocent Evans who is hanged for the crime (see Addresses in fiction.)

FAMOUS NAMES The original *Ocean's Eleven* starred five members of the Rat Pack – Peter Lawford, Frank Sinatra, Dean Martin, Sammy Davis Jr and Joey Bishop.

A GREATER SIGNIFICANCE The film *10 Rillington Place*, and the original 1961 book by Ludovic Kennedy were instrumental in changing British law to ban the death penalty.

Ocean's Eleven (1960)

Thief Danny Ocean, on parole from a New Jersey prison, wastes no time in planning and executing his next plan – a heist in which his accomplices, all World War II veterans, will simultaneously raid five Las Vegas casinos on New Year's Eve. But all does not go to plan and, after many crises, they fail to get the cash. The movie was remade in 2001 and was followed by *Ocean's Twelve* (2004) and *Ocean's Thirteen* (2007). In the 2018 *Ocean's 8* a team of women led by Debbie Ocean (Danny's sister) plan a diamond heist at the Met Gala in New York City.

12 Angry Men (1957)

Focused on the workings of an all-male jury in the trial of a teenager accused of stabbing his father to death, everything in this film revolves around the possible guilty verdict and its life extinguishing consequences. Tension continues to mount as arguments and juror votes swing to and fro until the finale.

The Dirty Dozen (1967)

In the run up to D-Day in 1944, Major Reisman is tasked with training a team of parachutists to cross into enemy territory and assassinate enemy characters resident in a country chateau. The twist in this US action thriller is that each of the 12 has a past convictions, including murder and rape, but participation will commute their sentences.

Apollo 13 (1995)

Knowing the outcome of the disastrous 1970 Apollo 13 moon mission led by Jim Lovell, is no barrier to the tension of this movie detailing the minute-by-minute drama of how NASA experts and the bravery of the crew succeeded in saving the lives of the astronauts aboard the stricken spacecraft.

21 Grams (2003)

Many plot lines, past, present and future, intertwine in this drama following a fatal hit-and-run motor accident featuring ex-convict Jack Jordan, mathematician Paul Rivers, his wife Mary who is in need of a heart transplant, and Christina Peck, a recovering drug addict. The title comes from the weight the body is said to lose at death when the soul departs.

101 Dalmatians (1961)

The original Disney animation tells the story of a litter stolen by the spiteful Crulla de Vil, whose aim is to turn the puppies' skins into fur coats. The brave parents, Pongo and Perdita, make it their mission to rescue their offspring and in doing so also rescue another 84 bought from pet shops – adding up to 101.

2001: A Space Odyssey (1968)

The sci-fi epic begins with the discovery of a black monolith by a tribe of early humans. Millions of years later we follow a voyage to Jupiter led by the 'live' computer HAL 9000. The many themes addressed include artificial intelligence, human evolution and extraterrestrial life. In the famous final scene the monolith reappears and the scientist Dr David Bowman is transformed into a foetus that floats in space above the earth.

COUNTING IN SONG

A NUMBER IN THE TITLE CAN CERTAINLY HELP MAKE A SONG MEMORABLE. THERE ARE FAR TOO MANY EXAMPLES TO MAKE A LIST INCLUSIVE – THIS IS A PERSONAL AND LARGELY VINTAGE SELECTION.

'One Fine Day' – 1963
Written for The Chiffons by Gerry Goffin and Carole King and inspired by the aria *Un bel di* from Puccini's opera *Madam Butterfly*.

'One Love' – 1965
'One love/One heart/Let's get together and feel alright', open the lyrics of Bob Marley & the Wailers' reggae anthem. It was included in the 'Exodus' album of 1977. Contained in the song is an interpretation of Curtis Mayfield's 'People Get Ready' written for The Impressions.

'It Takes Two' – 1966
Marvin Gaye and Kim Weston's hit, co-written with producer William 'Mickey' Stevenson working with Sylvia Moy. This timeless duet was successfully covered by both Rod Stewart and Tina Turner in 1990.

'Knock Three Times' – 1970
Performing with Tony Orlando on the original recording were Toni Wine and Linda November. The single is reputed to have sold 10,000 copies a day for 10 straight days in New York City.

'Three Steps to Heaven' – 1960
Co-written with his brother Bob and recorded by Eddie Cochran this became a posthumous UK number one following Cochran's death in a car accident in April 1960. The backing group was Buddy Holly's The Crickets.

'Three Times a Lady' – 1978
A number from the Commodores' album 'Natural High' and much covered by artists including Kenny Rogers (1980), Conway Twittie (1983) and Lionel Richie (2009).

'5-4-3-2-1' – 1964
When the group Manfred Mann – comprising Mann plus Tom McGuiness, Mike Hugg, Mike Vickers and Paul Jones – were asked to compose a theme tune for the ITV pop music programme *Ready Steady Go!*, this catchy number was the result and became an instant hit.

'Eight Days a Week' – 1964
Composed by John Lennon and Paul McCartney and based on a McCartney idea inspired by an overworked chauffeur, the title of this Beatles' standard has become a general expression for total commitment. It first appeared on the album 'Beatles for Sale'.

'9 to 5' – 1980
Written and originally performed by Dolly Parton for the film of the same name, the number received an Academy Award nomination. It has become an anthem for office workers on both sides of the Atlantic.

'Sixteen Going on Seventeen' (from *The Sound of Music*) **– 1959**
Justifying her relationship with Rolf (who is a year older), Leisl declares that she is old enough to make up her own mind. In the film it becomes a reprise after Rolf has rejected her. The songwriters were Don Roth and Timmy Tappan.

'Sweet Little Sixteen' – 1958
Chuck Berry's performance of his classic in the 1958 Newport Jazz Festival was included in the documentary film *Jazz on a Summer's Day*. It remains a perennial favourite.

'Only Sixteen' – 1959
The teenage classic by US singer-songwriter Sam Cooke and co-written with Lou Adler and Herb Alpert was successfully covered by Craig Douglas in the UK where it topped the charts.

'Twenty-Four Hours From Tulsa' – 1963
A song from the album 'Blue Gene' written by Burt Bacharach and Hal David, and epitomizing homesickness, it became a massive hit and signature tune for Gene Pitney and made him an international star.

'25 or 6 to 4' – 1970
Written by the American musician Robert Lamm, a founder member of Chicago, the title refers to Lamm's efforts to write in the early hours – at 25 or 26 minutes to 4 in the morning. It was originally recorded for the group's second album 'Chicago' with Peter Cetera on lead vocals.

'50 Ways to Leave Your Lover' – 1975
One of American singer-songwriter Paul Simon's best-known songs, from his studio album 'Still Crazy After All These Years', was written following Simon's divorce from his first wife Peggy Harper. It is a mistress's humorous advice to a husband on how to end a relationship.

'When I'm 64' – 1975
Originally written by Paul McCartney when only 16, and included in the Beatles' early set list, it was first recorded for inclusion in the 'Sgt Pepper's Lonely Hearts Club' album. It was scored by George Martin, who added clarinets to counteract the 'schmaltz factor' McCartney had identified and disliked.

'Route 66' – 1946
Bobby Troupe's 12-bar blues inspired by a cross America journey (see Roads to take) became a hit for Nat King Cole and his Trio. Bing Crosby with the Andrews Sisters also reached the charts with it in the same year. The many other artists with the song to their name include

Chuck Berry, The Rolling Stones and Dr Feelgood.

'99 Red Balloons' – 1983

In June 1982 guitarist Carlo Karges of the German group Nena was at a Rolling Stones concert in West Berlin when he saw balloons drifting in the air looking like UFOs and imagined them floating over into the city's Soviet east. The result was '99 *Luftballons*', an anti-war protest song. The original English language version (not a direct translation) with lyrics by Kevin McLea was released on the album '99 Luftballons' in 1984.

'2000 Light Years From Home' – 1967

With lyrics said to have been penned by Mick Jagger whilst in Brixton prison following his conviction for drug charges this psychedelic rock number was first released on the Stones' album 'Their Satanic Majesties Request' and is attributed to Jagger and Keith Richards.

JAZZ NUMBERS

ALTHOUGH MANY ARE TECHNICALLY SONGS, THESE NUMBERS ARE MARKED OUT BY BEING ESSENTIALS IN THE JAZZ REPERTOIRE.

'One Note Samba' – 1960

A bossa nova composed by the Brazilian composer Antônio Carlos Jobim, originally with lyrics by Newton Mendonça. It first appeared in João Gilberto's album '*O Amor, o Sorriso e a Flor*'.

'One O'Clock Jump' –1937

A 12-bar blues and jazz standard by Count Basie, assisted by Eddie Durham and Buster Smith who wrote down the riffs of band members. Basie played piano on the original recording with Herschel Evans and Lester Young on sax, Buck Clayton on trumpet and Walter Page on bass.

'Tea for Two' – 1925

Originally sung by Louise Groody and Jack Barker in the stage musical *No, No, Nanette,* and later in the 1950 film version by Doris Day and Gordon MacRae. The song has lasted down the years and become a jazz standard, notably performed by Thelonius Monk and Art Tatum.

'Three Little Words' – 1930

Accompanied by Duke Ellington's orchestra, The Rhythm Boys, including Bing Crosby, first recorded the number that was subsequently used in the soundtrack of the eponymous 1950 movie. The score was by Harry Ruby and lyrics by Bert Kalmar.

'Four' – 1954

Miles Davis remains credited with this standard first released on his 'Blue Haze' album though the alto saxophonist Eddie 'Cleanhead' Vinson has claimed ownership for the song. The lyrics begin 'Of the wonderful things that you get out of life there are four./And they may not be many but nobody needs any more'.

'Four on Six' – 1965

The title of this number by jazz guitarist Wes Montgomery is believed to refer to the movement of four fingers on six guitar strings. Montgomery is renowned for unusually plucking the strings with the side of his thumb.

'Take Five' – 1959

The catchy number so many associate with jazz was famously performed by the Dave Brubeck Quartet – originally at New York's Village Gate nightclub – and composed by Paul Desmond. In 1961 it became the highest selling jazz single of all time. The name comes from its unusual 5/4 meter.

'Seven Steps to Heaven' – 1963

Included in the up-tempo album of the same name by the Miles Davis Quintet this was a joint composition between trumpeter Davis and pianist and vibes player Victor Feldman. The Jon Hendricks lyrics include the chorus: 'One two three four five six seven,/that's heaven....

'26-2' – 1960

Originally recorded by John Coltrane the number was not released until 1970 on 'The Coltrane Legacy' album. It is based on Charlie Parker's tune 'Confirmation' with altered chords.

'500 Miles High' – 1973

Pianist Chick Corea originally performed his fusion number, combining jazz harmony and improvization with rhythm and blues, rock and funk with his band Return to Forever. The first verse of Neville Potter's lyrics runs:

Some day you'll look in to her eyes
Then there'll be no goodbyes
And yesterday will have gone
You'll find yourself in another space
500 miles high.

A MUSICAL MISCELLANY

NUMBERS HAVE SO MANY
ASSOCIATIONS WITH MUSIC – FROM THE
SIMPLE TO THE HIGHLY COMPLEX. JUST
A FEW EXAMPLES ARE INCLUDED HERE
TO GIVE A FLAVOUR OF THE RANGE
AFFORDED.

In musical notation the most obvious interval between notes is the octave. Named from the number eight, and known since the time of Pythagoras, it is generally defined as a series of eight notes occupying the interval between (and including) two notes, one having twice or half the frequency or vibration of the other. The easiest example is the C major scale, which is written as C D E F G A B C. Here the first and last Cs are an octave apart and sound essentially – and pleasingly – the same to the human ear. It is from variations on this simple concept that all musical composition has evolved.

Playing together

A full-size symphony or philharmonic orchestra consists of 70 to 100 musicians, divided into four basic sections: strings, woodwind, brass and percussion. A chamber or concert orchestra is smaller, with 50 or fewer players. The typical orchestra grew in size throughout the 18th and 19th centuries, reaching a peak with as many as 120 players, notably to perform the works of Richard Wagner and Gustav Mahler. Smaller groups of players, logically named duets, trios, quartets, quintets and so on, often specialize in particular types of music.

Numbered works

The assignment of opus numbers, meaning 'work' to musical compositions by Utalina and German composers began in the 15th and 16th centuries. By the 17th century numbering works in chronological order had become the norm. Various musicologists have created their own catalogues for specific composers of which the most famous include:

BWV (*Bach-Werke-Verzeichnis*) numbers – for Johann Sebastien Bach, assigned by Wolfgang Schmieder.

K or **KV** (*Köchel-Verzeichnis nummer*) – for Wolfgang Amadeus Mozart assigned by Ludwig Ritter von Köchel.

D – for Franz Schubert, as catalogued by Otto Erich Deutsch.

The instruments

In stringed instruments such as violins, violas, cellos and double basses usually four strings are plucked or stroked by a bow to generate sound, while the length of the string (and therefore the note) is altered by hand movements on a fingerboard. The guitar, with six strings, is broadly similar. The brilliant tones of the modern trumpet travel through about 2 m (6½ ft) of tubing bent into an oblong shape. The trombone is essentially a long brass tube folded back on itself rather like a giant paper clip, and has a slide which, when moved, creates notes by changing the length of its approximately 3 m (1 yard) of tubing. A pair of

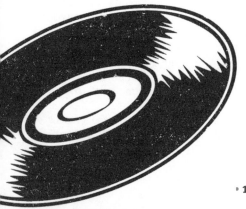

reeds helps to create the characteristic sounds of the oboe and bassoon; the clarinet and saxophone are single reed instruments.

There are 88 keys covering eight octaves on a standard piano keyboard, 52 white and 36 black, but the number can range from 96 down to 61 or even 37 on portable electric instruments. The piano's great musical versatility comes in part from its ability to play chords of up to 10 notes and two or more independent musical lines simultaneously.

On the record

In the early days of the phonograph discs played at a variety of speeds, usually between 60 and 130 rpm (revolutions per minute). By 1894 the United States Gramophone Company was advertising its single 7-in discs at 'about 70 rpm'. By the mid 1920s, 78 rpm became established as a norm, though for no apparent technical reason.

The '78' has persisted to the 21st century, but as the recording industry expanded, other formats were added. The first 'single', a 7-inch 45-rpm record, was released in the US by RCA Victor on 31 March, 1949. The song was 'Pee Wee the Piccolo' by Paul Wing. Midway between the single and the LP was the EP or extended play record, which played at 33⅓ rpm and was first produced by Columbia in June 1948.

IN SYMPHONY

As the symphony evolved it settled into a roughly standard form of four movements: 1. An allegro or sonata; 2. An adagio or other slow movement; 3. A minuet or trio; 4. An allegro, rondo or sonata.

The numbers of their symphonies help to define the great composers: Most prolific were Haydn (104) and Mozart (41). Among most famous are those of Beethoven (9), Mahler (9), Schubert (10), Dvorak (9), Mendelssohn (5), Shostakovich (15) and Tchaikovsky (6).

POETRY'S SECRETS REVEALED

UNLIKELY AS IT MAY SEEM, NUMBERS PLAY AN ESSENTIAL PART IN MAKING POETRY RESOUND IN OUR MINDS AND HEARTS. AND NUMBERS ARE VITAL TO VERSE SUCH AS THE SONNET, HAIKU AND LIMERICK.

The most basic element of rhyming poetry is the foot, which consists of two syllables. These can be stressed or unstressed, and the way in which this is done provides a poem's cadence. There are many ways in which the foot can be expressed, for example:

The iambic foot: a foot with two syllables, the first of which is not stressed. Shakespeare wrote a perfect example in the last two lines of his *Sonnet 18* (stressed syllables in capitals):

As LONG as MEN can BREATHE or EYES can SEE,
So LONG lives THIS and THIS gives LIFE to THEE.

The trochee is the reverse of the iambic foot with the first syllable stressed. Again Shakespeare does it perfectly in the opening of *Macbeth* when the witches chant:

DOUBLE, double, TOIL and trouble.

In the spondee a foot has two syllables, both of them stressed. This pattern occurs in Henry Wadsworth Longfellow's *Song of Hiawatha*:

By the shore of Gitche Gumee,
By the shining BIG–SEA–WAter,
At the DOORWAY of his WIGWAM,...
All the air was full of FRESHNESS,

DREAM INSPIRED

Kubla Khan, Samuel Taylor Coleridge's famous poem, begins:

In Xanadu did Kubla Khan
A stately pleasure dome
decree ...

Believed to have been inspired by an opium-fuelled dream in 1797 the poem that was first published in 1816 is just 54 lines long. Coleridge had, on waking, more than 200 lines in his head but was interrupted in committing them to paper and forgot the remainder.

The anapest is a foot with three syllables, the first two of them stressed, the third unstressed. Lord Byron used this form in *The Destruction of Sennacherib*:

The AsSYRian came DOWN like the WOLF on the FOLD,
And his Cohorts were GLEAming in PURPLE and GOLD;

The dactyl is a foot with three syllables, the first unstressed, the second and third stressed.

Measuring the feet

Then comes metre, which is a measurement of the number of feet a line of poetry contains. These range from the monometre with a single foot, through the dimeter (2 feet); trimeter (3 feet); tetrameter (4 feet); pentameter (5

THE MATHEMATICIAN'S SLANT

There is a strong affinity between mathematics and poetry, as exemplified by writers from Omar Kahayyám to Lewis Carroll. In 2009 contemporary poets were invited to write what was called the 'Golden Fib', a poetic form of 6 lines and 20 syllables based on the Fibonacci series (see Fibonacci) which begins 1, 1, 2, 3, 5, 8. The original, devised by the American screenwriter Gregory K Pincus runs:

> One Small,
> Precise,
> Poetic,
> Spiralling mixture:
> Math plus poetry yields the Fib.

For the Nobel Prize winning Polish poet Wislaw Szymborska (1923–2012), the digits of π proved the subject of a memorable verse which she begins:

> The admirable number pi: three point one four one.
> All the following digits are also initial
> five nine two because it never ends.
> It can't be comprehended six five three five at a glance.
> eight nine by calculation.
> seven nine or imagination .....

feet); hexameter (6 feet); heptameter (7 feet); and the octameter (8 feet). In the 8th century BCE Homer almost certainly used the hexameter in his *Odyssey* and *Iliad*.

In a poem, feet and metre combine. So that in the well known verse by Elizabeth Barrett Browning: 'How do I love thee?/ Let me count the ways' each line has five feet and each of these feet is an iamb, making the form an iambic pentameter.

The sonnet

Named from the Italian *sonetto*, (which in turn comes from *sonet*, a little poem in Old Provençal and *sonus*, the Latin for sound) the sonnet was already defined as a 14-line poem by the 13th century and was adopted by English poets such as John Milton. The Italian form is typically written in iambic pentameter and divided into two parts, the first of 8 lines and the second of 6. Much better known is the Shakespearean form, as in Sonnet 116 penned in 1609:

> Let me not to the marriage of true minds
> Admit impediments. Love is not love
> Which alters when it alteration finds,
> Or bends with the remover to remove.
> O no! it is an ever-fixed mark
> That looks on tempests and is never shaken;
> It is the star to every wand'ring bark,
> Whose worth's unknown, although his height be taken.
> Love's not Time's fool, though rosy lips and cheeks
> Within his bending sickle's compass come;
> Love alters not with his brief hours and weeks,
> But bears it out even to the edge of doom.
> If this be error and upon me prov'd,
> I never writ, nor no man ever lov'd.

In this form there are three quatrains (groups of four lines) and a final couplet. The scheme of the rhyme runs A-B-AB, C-D-C-D, E-F-E-F, GG.

The haiku and limerick

The haiku, which dates to 9th century Japan when it was called *hokku*, is a poetic way to express a pair of juxtaposed thoughts, often focused on the nature and our thoughts and feelings. It does this in a structured form consisting of 17 *moras*, or syllables, arranged in the sequence 5-7-5. In their early conception, haikus would be written by more than one person, each contributing a line in turn.

The poet Basho Matsuo was a master of the haiku. These are examples he wrote in the 1600s:

An old silent pond...
A frog jumps into the pond,
splash! Silence again.

Autumn moonlight—
a worm digs silently
into the chestnut.

Lightning flash—
what I thought were faces
are plumes of pampas grass.

Although it was made famous by the poet and artist Edward Lear in *A Book of Nonsense* published in 1846, the limerick is thought to have had its birth in medieval France in the 11th century as in this verse (in modern spelling):

The lion is wondrous strong
And full of the wiles of woe;
And whether he play
Or take his prey
He cannot do by slay.

The key features are the five lines, with the first, second and fifth written in trimester and the third and fourth in dimeter form.

Of the Lear limericks this is one of the most famous:

There was an Old Man with a beard,
Who said, 'It is just as I feared!
Two Owls and a Hen,
Four Larks and a Wren,
Have all built their nests in my beard!

THE BEAUTIFUL GAME

FOOTBALL, OR SOCCER AS IT IS KNOWN IN THE USA, IS A HUGELY POPULAR SPECTATOR SPORT AND THE ENGLISH PREMIER LEAGUE IS TELEVISED WORLDWIDE. THE SPORT, PROPERLY CALLED ASSOCIATION FOOTBALL, IS ALSO FULL OF NUMBERS OF ALL KINDS AND TODAY MANAGERS KNOW HOW FAR EACH PLAYER RUNS DURING A GAME AND HOW MANY PASSES THEY HAVE MADE.

There are 11 players in a football team, as established in 1848 when Cambridge University made the first real attempt to codify the rules. Before then there might be many more, all frantically – and violently – trying to kick the ball and each other. Based on the Cambridge rules the formal laws were first drawn up by the Yorkshire-born London solicitor and sportsman Ebenezer Cobb Morley and approved by the newly founded Football Association (FA) on 8 December 1863.

Professionally, football is played on a pitch that must be between 90 m (100 yards) and 120 m (130 yards) long and between 45 m (50 yards) and 90 m (100 yards) wide. The ball used in leagues and international competitions, including the World Cup is known as a 'size 5'; it is 69–71 cm (27–28 in) in circumference and weighs 400–450 g (14–16 oz). In the past penalties were always taken from the 12-yard spot within the 18-yard box, but now it is the 11-metre spot or in German the *Elfmeter Schoss*.

Orgnizing the line up

A team of 11 players sounds simple to organize, but teams who have won the World Cup have lined up in at least 12 different formations since the tournament's inception in 1930. The numbers are arranged starting with the players nearest the goalkeeper:

2-3-5	The original 'W' formation Uruguay, 1930 and Italy, 1934, 1938
4-3-3	Uruguay 1950, Brazil 1962 and Germany 2014
4-2-4	Brazil 1958, 1970, West Germany 1974 and Argentina 1978
3-5-2	Argentina 1986
5-3-2	West Germany 1990
3-2-2-3	West Germany 1954
4-3-2-1	France 1998
4-4-2	England 1966, Brazil 1994
4-4-1-1	Italy 2006
4-2-3-1	Spain 2010
3-4-3	Brazil 2002

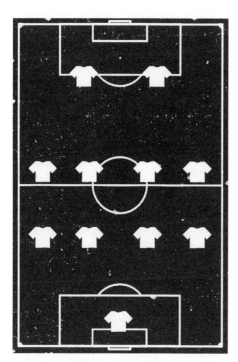

The 4-4-2 formation

The number on the shirt

When organized football began no substitutes were allowed; it became legal throughout the game in 1958 with one being allowed, plus another for an injured goalkeeper. In 1988 it increased to two from five 'on the bench' and in 1994 was raised to two from five plus one (specifically an injured goalkeeper). A year later the rule became any three from five. In some cup competitions a fourth sub is allowed if extra time is played. The general rule is due to be raised to three from seven in 2019.

The introduction of substitutes was instrumental in changing the player numbering system. Originally players were numbered 1 to 11, according to their playing position (see The oval ball game). So number 9 was the centre forward, 7 and 11 the right and left wings respectively, and number 5 the centre half. The first substitute was always number 12 and the second 14.

However with clubs now having squads of 25 players, and even using numbers as large as 99, the actual number has much less significance, although some players clearly identify with certain numbers, particularly 3, 5, 7, 9, 10, 11 and even 17 or 23. When David Beckham went to Real Madrid in 2003, his number 7 shirt was already taken by Raul (Raul Gonzalez Blanco) so he chose 23 as a nice prime number which, perhaps significantly, was also

the number of basketball's big star Michael Jordan.

In 1970, long before squad numbers, the Dutchman Johan Cruyff unexpectedly turned out for Ajax against PSV Eindhoven wearing number 14. He had given his usual number 9 to colleague Gerrie Muhren when the midfielder had failed to find his usual 7. The first shirt Cruyff picked from the basket was 14. A week later Cruyff said to his teammate (much to the disdain of the authorities): 'Gerrie, PSV went so well, let's just play with the same numbers.' The rest is history.

Scores, points and records

Until 1981, in English leagues only two points were awarded for a win and one for a draw. This meant that in the top division the total number of points available was always $22 \times 21 \times 2 \times 2 = 1,848$ points. With 3 points for a win and only 20 teams in the Premier League (begun in 1992), the maximum number of points available is now $20 \times 19 \times 2 \times 3 = 1,140$. But if all games were drawn, the total points would only be 760. Teams aiming to avoid relegation from the Premier League will aim for a minimum of 40 points or more although in some years 35 is sufficient.

The record for the biggest win is Manchester United's 9–0 victory against Ipswich Town at Old Trafford on 4 March 1995. Tottenham Hotspur are the only other club to have scored nine goals in a Premier League game, beating Wigan Athletic 9–1 at White Hart Lane on 22 November 2009. On Boxing Day, 26 December 1963, Blackburn Rovers beat West Ham United 8–2 at Upton Park. But clearly they must have over celebrated, because West Ham won the return fixture 3–1 two days later at Ewood Park.

England's Geoff Hurst remains the only player to have scored a hat-trick in a World Cup Final when he scored three goals against West Germany on 30 July 1966. In the World Cup of 2014 Brazil lost to Germany 7–1 at the Estadio Minerao in Minas Gerais. The memory of that game has now replaced that of the 1950 Final, when Brazil lost 1–2 to

PREMIER LEAGUE WINNERS Since its inception in 1992, 49 clubs have competed for the title and many have seen multiple successes. The only six winners to the end of the 2017/18 season are: Manchester United (13), Chelsea (5), Arsenal (3), Manchester City (3), Blackburn Rovers (1) and Leicester City (1).

Uruguay in the Maracana, Rio de Janeiro, after which Brazil felt obliged to change the colour of their kit. Most of the record 199,854 spectators went home disappointed.

Paid to play

After World War I professional footballers in Britain received a maximum weekly wage of £10 and in 1920 the Football League Management Committee proposed a reduction to £9 when there was a call for strike action. However, large numbers of players resigned from the Player's Union and the £9 was imposed. The following year it was reduced to £8 for a 37-week playing season and £6 for the 15-week close season.

Despite the efforts of the Players' Union, there was no other change until 1945 when the maximum close season weekly wage was increased to £7. Subsequently gradual increases were granted, keeping footballers' incomes roughly double a typical industrial wage. Faced in 1961 with the prospect of strike action the maximum wage was abolished and Johnny Haynes, the England captain, became the first £100-per-week player.

Since then, the average footballer's weekly wage in England's top division has skyrocketed. While George Best was paid £1,000 a week by Manchester United in 1968, by 2016 the club were paying Paul Pogba around £320,000 a week. Other top paid players around the world include Alexis Sanchez reported to earn £600,000 a week, also at United in 2018. Worldwide, the highest paid player in the 2017–18 season was Lionel Messi of Barcelona whose earnings reputedly totalled £40.5 million or just under £779,000 a week.

Transfer Fees

Since Alf Common was transferred from Middlesbrough to Sunderland in 1905 for £1,000, the football transfer world has undergone a huge evolution. In 1951, £34,500 would have bought Sheffield Wednesday either 78 kg (172 lb) of gold, or John 'Jackie' Sewell from Notts County – arguably the first footballer to be declared worth more than his weight in gold.

The first million pound footballer was Trevor Francis when signed by Brian Clough in 1979 for Nottingham Forest from Birmingham City. At the time of going to press the record transfer fee – which is almost certain to be broken within months – was held by the Brazilian forward Neymar, who moved from Barcelona to Paris Saint-Germain for £198 million. His full name is Neymar da Silva Santos Junior.

THE HERO KEEPER

Before substitutes there are many stories of a gallant ten men either hanging onto a lead, or bravely fighting on to an almost inevitable defeat. Most renowned is Bert Trautmann the Manchester City goalkeeper who broke his neck in the 1956 Cup Final against Birmingham City, and played on for the last 17 minutes, making several fine saves when he could easily have died. His team won 3–1. Remarkably the German born Trautmann had stayed in England after being held in a prisoner of war camp during World War II and rejecting Nazi ideology.

THE OVAL BALL GAME – RUGBY FOOTBALL

IT IS PROBABLY A MYTH THAT WILLIAM WEBB ELLIS, A PUPIL AT RUGBY SCHOOL, PICKED UP THE BALL AND RAN WITH IT DURING A GAME OF 'REGULAR' FOOTBALL TO INVENT THE GAME OF RUGBY, BUT ITS FIRST COMPILED LAWS WERE CERTAINLY WRITTEN AT THE SCHOOL IN 1845.

Rugby, or rugby union as it is properly called to distinguish it from rugby league (see below) is played with an oval ball measuring 280–300 mm in length, 740–770 mm in circumference lengthwise and 580–620 mm in circumference measured round the full width. At each end of the 100 × 70 m pitch, which is marked with key lines at 22 and 10 m from the halfway line, are a pair of goal posts 6 to 13.5 m tall placed 5.6 m apart and linked with a crossbar placed 3m from the ground. These dimensions are now always expressed as metric, not imperial measurements.

The game consists of two halves of 40 minutes, the clock being stopped when play pauses for injuries, substitutions or other interruptions. Each team starts the match with 15 players on the field – eight forwards (the pack) and seven backs – and seven or eight substitutes. Their usual shirt numbers are shown in the diagram. The forwards are organized in three rows with the number 8 between the two locks. The backs are spread out behind the forwards, starting with the scrum half. The centres and the wings are often known as the three-quarters.

Scoring points

In rugby union 5 points are scored for a try, when the ball is put down over the opponent's line, plus 2 for a conversion in which the ball is kicked between the posts and over the crossbar. There are 3 for a penalty kick or drop goal. Of all the greatest points scored in the history of the game most have played at number 9 or 10.

The following players have scored more than 1,000 points in their international careers:

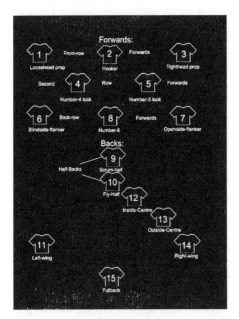

Rugby union positions

Player (Number)	Country	Caps	Tries	Conversions	Penalties	Drop goals	TOTAL points
Daniel Carter (10)	New Zealand	112	29	293	281	8	1,598
Jonny Wilkinson (10)	England and British Lions	97	7	169	255	36	1,246
Neil Jenkins (10, 12, 15)	Wales and British Lions	87	11	131	246	10	1,090
Ronan O'Gara (10)	Ireland and British Lions	130	16	176	202	15	1,083
Diego Dominguez	Argentina	76	9	133	209	20	1,010

INTERNATIONAL NUMBERS

In the spring of each year, European teams from England, Wales, Scotland, Ireland, France and Italy compete in the six nations tournament. Originally a four nations affair involving just the home countries, France joined in 1900, though was later excluded for poor discipline and results. However from 1939 they became permanent members of the five nations. Italy became the sixth competitor in 2000.

CRITICAL AREA

The key area for attack/defence, once known as the '25' (yards) is now the 22 since rugby is now metric. However the line originally 5 yards from the touchline and try line is still the '5'.

MORE RUGBY UNION RECORDS

- The New Zealand openside flanker No 7 Richie McCaw is the most capped top tier player with 148 caps.
- In 2016 the New Zealand All Blacks set a record of 18 consecutive test wins. This was equalled by England on 11 March 2017 with a win over Scotland at Twickenham.
- The highest scoring international match was Hong Kong's 164–13 victory over Singapore on 27 October 1994.

Rugby league

Originally, rugby was a purely amateur sport, but rugby league originated in 1895 as a professional, subsequently faster game played by teams of 13. Compared with rugby union the scrum is smaller, omitting the two flankers, and only four substitutes are allowed. At the height of its popularity in 1954 a record 102,569 spectators watched the replay of the Challenge Cup final between Warrington and Halifax at the Odsal Stadium in Bradford, Yorkshire.

From 1966 a rule was introduced allowing the team in possession of the ball three plays, so that on the fourth tackle a scrum must be formed. This was increased to six tackles in 1972. As for points, 4 are awarded for a try, 2 for a conversion or penalty and just 1 for a drop goal.

THE GAME OF GOLF

GOLF IS A GAME THAT DEPENDS GREATLY ON NUMBERS FOR ITS MAGIC, AS PLAYERS OF ALL ABILITIES AIM TO COMPLETE THE COURSE IN THE FEWEST POSSIBLE SHOTS. TO EQUAL THE STANDARD NUMBER OF SHOTS FOR THE COURSE, ADJUSTED ACCORDING TO YOUR HANDICAP IF NECESSARY, IS TO SHOOT A PAR.

There is no standard golf course length, as the design varies with local geography, but courses generally comprise of either 18 or 9 holes. The typical length of holes is:

Par 3 – 250 yards (230 m) and below
Par 4 – 251–450 yards (230–411 m)
Par 5 – 451–690 yards (412–631 m)

An 18-hole golf course will have typically 3 par 3 holes, 12 par 4s and 3 par 5s making its overall length between 6,000 and 7,000 yards (5,500 to 6,500 m). To hole the ball in one shot under par is a birdie, two below par is an eagle and three under par an albatross. One over par is a bogie, two over a double bogie and three over a triple bogie.

The ball and clubs

The dynamics of the golf ball depend greatly on its many dimples, which reduce the amount of drag and accentuate the lift, adding around 115 per cent distance per shot. Dimples can vary from 252 to 500 per ball, with an optimum of 350 to 450. Golf ball manufacturers tend to produce dimple patterns by using the highest order of symmetry, dividing the ball into 20 identical triangles. Competition golf balls must not weigh less than 45.93 grams (1.62 oz), while their diameter

and above, which come in five types, the maximum loft being 64-68°. Today's club golfers favour the hybrid, a cross between a wood and an iron, and golfers of all standards will need a reliable putter. No golfer is allowed more than 14 clubs in their bag, and these cannot be changed during a round.

Forms of the game

There are two distinct forms of golf, with different scoring systems. In stroke play, players count the total number of strokes taken over each 18 holes, and the total is adjusted according to the player's handicap. The higher the handicap (up to a maximum of 36, or two shots per hole for women) the more 'extra' shots the player is allowed. A 'scratch' player effectively has a handicap of zero. In match play, a player can win, lose or halve an individual hole, again with the handicap being taken into consideration. Towards the end of the round, a player winning by 3 holes, with only 2 still to play, will be adjudged to have won by '3 and 2'.

cannot be less than 42.67 mm (1.68 in). Their shape must be as close as possible to a symmetric sphere.

There is also a numbering system for clubs, ranging from 1 to 9. A number 9 iron (now made of a steel alloy) is the most steeply angled at 44-45°, and used for relatively short pitches – the number decreasing with the angle. The 1,2 and 3 are known as woods whatever their composition. Other types of club are the wedges, which with angles of 47-48°

Dreams and records

Golfers of all abilities dream of the hole in one, usually only possible on a par 3 hole, even though it means buying drinks for everyone in the clubhouse afterwards. Among the most memorable holes in one are those of 71-year-old American Gene Sarazen at the 1973 Open and Earl Dietering of Memphis,

VARIATIONS ON A THEME

There are many other forms of competition in which golfers play in pairs. In foursomes, each pair only uses one ball and players strike it alternately. In fourballs, each player plays his own ball, and the winner of the hole is determined on the better ball.

Tennessee, aged 78, who is the oldest person to have shot two holes in one in a single round. In Rio de Janiero on 11 August 2016, British golfer Justin Rose became the first Olympian to score a hole in one and the first ever winner of an Olympic gold medal in his sport.

The world record for the longest drive in professional play is held by American Mike Austin, who drove 515 yards (471 m) at the Winterwood Course in Las Vegas in 1974. The longest known putt is attributed to 66-year-old Scotsman Fergus Muir, who holed a monster of 375 ft (114 m) at the St Andrew's Eden Course in 2001. On 7 August 2016 American professional Jim Furyk became the first, and as yet the only golfer on the PGA tour, to record a round of 58.

THE FAVOURITE HOLE

For many club golfers, the most important hole is the 19th, as the clubhouse serving the food and drink is often called.

THROWING DARTS

FOR THOSE WHO LOVE NUMBERS THERE ARE FEW GAMES TO BEAT DARTS, WHICH CAN BE PLAYED AT HOME OR ENJOYED AT A PUB OR CLUB. AS WELL AS ACCURATE THROWING, QUICK - FIRE ABILITY WITH ARITHMETIC HELPS HUGELY IN CALCULATING A WINNING STRATEGY.

The standard dartboard contains 20 sectors, joining a bull's eye in the centre which scores 50 for the inner circle and 25 for its outer ring. Numbers are arranged so that low ones are adjacent to high ones. Within the board are two narrow rings, an inner one which scores treble the sectoral value, and an outer which scores double the sectoral value. This means that the possible scores from throwing a single dart are all the numbers from 1 to 20, plus 20, 21, 22, 24, 25, 26, 27, 28, 30, 32, 33, 34, 36, 38, 39, 40, 42, 45, 48, 50, 51, 54, 57, and the maximum of triple 20 which is 60.

In a game of darts each player throws three darts per turn. The most common scoring is to work from a start number of 501 (but it can be 701 or even 1,001) down to exactly zero, but it is compulsory to end with a double. In 501 darts a perfect round can be completed in 9 darts. Assuming that all of the first 6 darts score treble 20 (180) then 141 is required for the final 3. The three usual ways in which this can be achieved, with a compulsory final double are:

- treble 20 (60), treble 19 (57), double 12 (24)
- treble 20 (60), treble 15 (45), double 18 (36)
- treble 17 (51), treble 18 (54), double 18 (36)

The highest score possible with three darts is 180, nicknamed a 'ton 80', which happens when all three darts land in the triple 20 – an achievement announced exuberantly by referees in televised and tournament games.

The dimensions of darts

A regulation board is 17¾ in (451 mm) in diameter and should be hung with the centre of the bull's eye 5 ft 8 in (1.73 m) from the floor, a height considered eye level for 6-ft (1.8 m) man. The oche, the line behind which the thrower must stand, should be 7ft 9¼ in (2.37 m) from the board face. Modern high-tech darts have steel points either 32 or 41 mm long.

POWER PLAY

Phil 'The Power' Taylor, who retired from professional play in 2018 is considered the world's all time best. He won 216 professional tournaments, including 16 World Championships, 8 of them consecutively from 1995 to 2002.

CRICKET – BAT ON BALL

THE GAME OF CRICKET, WHICH CAN NOW LAST FROM AROUND FOUR HOURS TO FIVE DAYS, IS A STATISTICIANS DELIGHT FROM THE MOMENT TWO OPENING BATSMEN AND 11 PLAYERS ON THE OPPOSING SIDE TAKE TO THE FIELD, ONE OF WHOM WILL PLAY AS THE WICKETKEEPER.

The set up for cricket is a field whose perimeter – the boundary – is marked with a rope or similar. At its centre is a pitch measuring 22 yards (20 m); at each end of this is a set of wickets consisting of three 28-inch (70-cm) stumps, topped with a pair of bails.

Balls are bowled in overs of six balls each to batsmen (also called batters) whose aim is to score runs which can be acquired as singles, when the two batters cross, or in boundaries – four for a ball that crosses the boundary on the ground, or six for one that does so without touching. The aim of the bowler is to get the batters out by various means, which may or may not (as with a catch) involve removal of the bails.

The laws of cricket state that the bat, which is usually made of white willow, must have a blade no wider than 4¼ in (106 mm). Total bat length, including the handle must be no more than 38 in (95 cm). There is no restriction on weight, but a normal bat weighs between 2½ and 3 lb (1.13 and 1.36 kg). The hard leather-covered ball, with a prominent seam made of six rows of stitches, has a standard circumference of 9 in (22.9 cm).

Today cricket is played in a variety of formats. The longest are the five-day international or Test Matches and the three or four-day county or regional matches, in which each side may bat and field twice. In 2018 there were two limited over one-day formats: 50 overs per side and 20 per side or TwentyTwenty.

Records galore

Cricket offers great scope for statistics, especially runs scored by teams, individuals and 'stands' between pairs of batters, and the numbers of wickets and catches taken. In Test Match (international) cricket, 26 players are listed as having scored over 300 runs in an innings, but only four have done so twice, namely Don Bradman of Australia, Verinder Sehwag of India, and Chris Gayle and Brian Lara of the West Indies. Brian Lara holds the current world record score of 400 not out. Of these players, however, the legendary Sir Donald Bradman has the highest average in Test Matches, of 99.76 (his total runs divided by his number of dismissals). If he had not been bowled out for a duck (nought) in his last ever game, his average would have been over 100.

The batsmen with the highest aggregate number of runs in Test Cricket to date are:

Batsman	Country	Aggregate runs
Sachin Tendulkar	India	15,921
Ricky Ponting	Australia	13,378
Jacques Kallis	South Africa	13,289
Rahul Dravid	India	13,288
Kumar Sangakkara	Sri Lanka	12,400

In Test Matches, two players have hit 28 runs in a single over – Brian Lara of the West Indies and George Bailey of Australia. In a three-day game between the West Indies and Glamorgan, Gary Sobers' extraordinary hitting of Glamorgan's Malcolm Nash for six sixes in one over on 31 August 1968 is the stand out achievement. Many batting feats have also been accomplished in the short forms of the game. In a TwentyTwenty international in April 2016, for example, Carlos Brathwaite of the West Indies hit England's Ben Stokes for four sixes in the first four balls of the last over to win the match, when an England victory had earlier looked almost certain.

In terms of bowling, only six players have taken more than 500 wickets in Test cricket:

Player	Country	Number of wickets
Muttiah Muralitharan	Sri Lanka	800
Shane Warne	Australia	708
Anil Kumble	India	619
Glenn McGrath	Australia	563
James Anderson	England	540
Courtney Walsh	West Indies	519

WHEN RAIN STOPS PLAY

When the weather interrupts one-day cricket it is now possible to decide on a fair winner using the Duckworth-Lewis method, a mathematical formulation devised by two cricket-loving statisticians, Frank Duckworth and Tony Lewis and designed to calculate the target score for the team batting second. It was first used officially on 1 January 1997 in a match between Zimbabwe and England.

Muttiah Muralitharan has taken 5 wickets in an innings on 67 occasions, and 10 wickets in a match on 22 occasions, making him Test cricket's most consistent wicket taker. An equally redoubtable record was set in July 1956, when England played Australia at Old Trafford and England's bowler, Jim Laker took 9 for 37 (that is 9 wickets taken whilst conceding only 37 runs) in the first innings and 10 for 53 in the second, making a total of 19 for 90 for the match.

ALL IN ONE VOLUME

For lovers of cricket statistics, there is no better source than *The Wisden Cricketer's Almanack*, known simply as Wisden, which has been published every year since 1864 when it was first compiled by cricketer John Wisden. However it does not include details of one-day cricket matches, which are not classified as 'first class'.

In 2018 England's bowler Anya Shrubsole became the first woman ever to feature on the front cover. Sensationally she took 5 wickets in 19 balls and had overall figures of 6 for 46 to help secure her team the 2017 World Cup.

ON COURT – THE GAME OF TENNIS

FROM A NUMBERS POINT OF VIEW, IT IS THE SCORING SYSTEM THAT MAKES TENNIS SO INTERESTING. AND EVEN WITH THE INTRODUCTION OF TIE BREAKS SOME MAMMOTH SCORES HAVE BEEN ACCUMULATED IN THE MAJOR SO-CALLED 'GRAND SLAM' TOURNAMENTS. The rather bizarre use of love, 15, 30, 40, deuce and advantage tends to obscure the fact that to win a game a tennis player simply needs 4 points, and to have won 2 more points than the opponent. Or, if players on each side of the net reach 3 points (deuce or 40 all) a player still needs to win two more points than the opponent.

The origins of the system probably date to medieval France where a clock face was used on court with a quarter move of the hand to indicate scores of 15, 30, 45 and finally 60, when the game ended. To accommodate deuce or equality (still *egalité* in French tennis), with 10 being awarded each time, the 45 was put back to 40. If the scores were

still equal then the clock would be put back to 40 again.

To win a set, a player must win 6 games, and have won 2 games more than their opponent. If, as often happens, the score reaches 6-6, a tie break is played in which the winner is the first player to reach 7 points, but with play continuing until one player is two points ahead of the other. In the 5-set matches played in major competitions, including the Grand Slams (which take place in Australia, France, the USA and Wimbledon in the UK), there is no tie break in the fifth set. All of this means that it is perfectly possible for a player who has won fewer games and points to triumph in the match.

A matter of size

A standard tennis court for both single and doubles must measure 78 ft (23.77 m) in length. A width of 27 ft (8.23m) is required for singles and 36 feet (10.97m) for doubles. The posts at the net ends must be 42 in (1.07 m) high and the net 36 in (0.914 m) at the centre.

As for balls, the International Tennis Federation (ITF) defines the official diameter as 6.54 to 6.86 cm (2.57 to 2.70 in) and with weights from 56.0 to 59.4 g (1.98 to 2.10 oz). The racquet has come a long way since the original wood and elastic rope version of the 1500s and is now made of materials including carbon and glass fibre, titanium and boron. Officially, the frame must not exceed 29 in (73.7 cm) in overall length, including the handle. The head width, which has increased massively over the years, must be no more than 12.5 in (31.7 cm) and the hitting surface no more than 15.5 in (39.4 cm) in length and 11.5 in (29.2 cm) wide.

THE LONGEST MATCH

Today's top players are in such good condition that a five-set match can last for four or five hours. The longest on record, taking 11 hours 5 minutes, over three separate days of play, was played at Wimbledon in 2010, when John Isner of USA defeated Nicholas Mahut of France 6-4, 3-6, 6-7, 7-6, 70-68. Unsurprisingly Isner lost his match in the next round.

The world's finest
Increasingly, tennis has being dominated by a few top players. These are the top all time Grand Slam singles winners to date.

Men	Country	Australian	French	Wimbledon	USA	Total
Roger Federer	Switzerland	6	1	8	5	20
Rafael Nadal	Spain	1	11	2	3	17
Pete Sampras	USA	2	0	7	5	14
Roy Emerson	Australia	6	2	2	2	12
Novak Djokovic	Serbia	6	1	3	2	12
Bjorn Borg	Sweden	0	6	5	0	11
Rod Laver	Australia	3	2	4	2	11

Women	Country	Australian	French	Wimbledon	USA	Total
Margaret Court	Australia	11	5	3	5	24
Serena Williams	USA	7	3	7	6	23
Steffi Graf	Germany	4	6	7	5	22
Helen Wills	USA	0	4	8	7	19
Chris Evert	USA	2	7	3	6	18
Martina Navratilova	Czech Republic/ USA	3	2	9	4	18
Billie Jean King	USA	1	1	6	4	8

SNOOKER AND OTHER CUE GAMES

THE SPORT OF KNOCKING COLOURED BALLS INTO THE POCKETS PLACED AROUND A TABLE COVERED WITH GREEN WOOLLEN CLOTH OR BAIZE IS POPULAR WORLDWIDE. APART FROM THE GAMES' BEAUTIFUL GEOMETRY, THEY ARE NUMERICALLY INTRIGUING.

International or 'English' snooker is its most widely enjoyed form. A full-sized table measures 11 ft 8½ in × 5 ft 10 in (3.569 × 1.778 m), but is commonly referred to as 12 × 6. There is a pocket at each corner and one half way along each side. The height of the table, from the floor to the top of the cushion rail should be 34 in (85 cm).

When set up for a frame, as a round is known, 15 red balls are placed in a triangle, and yellow, green, brown, blue, pink and black balls are placed on their own spots. The white ball is the cue ball – the one that has to be hit. The method of play is to pot a red ball, followed by a colour, which is replaced on the table, then another red and so on. When all the reds have been pocketed the colours are pocketed in order. Potting a red scores 1 point. Potting colours score: 2 (yellow), 3 (green), 4 (brown), 5 (blue), 6 (pink) or 7 (black). The maximum possible break on a full size table is 147, that is 15 × 1 reds + 15 × 7 blacks plus 27 for the remaining colours.

At a certain point in the game, it may be clear that a player cannot win but they may have a chance to snooker their opponent by 'hiding' the cue ball, so preventing a direct hit on a ball. If, for instance a player declares that after potting a red he is going to try for the black but instead hits the yellow then his opponent scores 4 points (the minimum penalty). If he were to hit the pink then the penalty would be 6 points. If he potted the yellow then the opponent would score 3.

Before and after

Snooker developed from billiards, a much older two-player game already known in the 15th century and played on the same sized table. The English version is played with a two white cue balls, one marked with a black dot, and a red object ball. Each player uses a different cue ball and points are scored as follows:

• 185 •

• **2 points:** cannon – striking the cue ball so that it hits, in any order, the other cue ball and the red ball on the same shot.
• **3 points:** winning hazard (potting) – striking the red ball with the cue ball so that the red goes into the pocket. Or for 2 points – striking the other cue ball with your own and putting it in a pocket.
• **3 points:** losing hazard – 3 points for striking your cue ball so that it hits another ball then goes into a pocket; 2 points if the other cue ball was hit first. Or • **2 points:** if the red and the other cue ball are hit simultaneously.
The maximum points that can be scored in one shot is 10.

Aiming for the 8-ball

Pool was developed in North America in the early 1900s, the most common variant being the 8-ball game played with a cue ball and 15 so-called object balls numbered from 1 to 15. One player aims to pocket the balls numbered 1 to 7 (solid colour balls), the other those numbered 9 to 15 (striped balls). The player pocketing either group first is then allowed to pocket the 8-ball and if successful is the winner. At the start of the game the balls are placed in a triangle with the 8-ball in the centre and with a stripe ball in one of the base corners and a solid ball in the other.

A losing sentiment

The expression to be 'behind the 8-ball' or in a difficult or losing position comes from the losing position in pool. A player will lose the game if they pot the 8 ball before all their other balls or if they hit the 8 ball off the table.

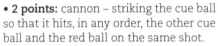

THE GAME OF BASEBALL

AMERICA'S NATIONAL GAME, WHICH WAS DEVELOPED FROM THE ENGLISH GAME OF ROUNDERS BY 18TH-CENTURY SETTLERS, IS A BOON TO THOSE WHO LOVE NUMBERS AS MUCH AS SPORT.
Each baseball teams consists of nine players, the aim being to score the most runs as each team bats and fields in turn. The game is divided into nine periods of play – the innings – each split into two halves with teams batting and fielding in turn. To end a half a team must succeed in putting three players of the batting team out. The batter, equipped with a bat not more than 42 in (107 cm) long and 2¾ in (77 mm) wide at its thickest point aims to hit the leather-covered, cork-cored ball, which weighs between 5 and 5½ oz (142–156 g) and is 2⅞ in (73 mm) in diameter.

The baseball playing area or pitch covers roughly 2 acres and incorporates an infield, the diamond, 90 ft (27 m) square on which are placed the three bases; in its centre is the spot occupied by the pitcher. The batter stands at the outer point of the diamond on the left hand or outer part of the base plate. Behind him is the catcher. The two sides of the square nearest to the batter are foul lines. Beyond it is the outfield split in half by the arc-shaped grassline.

Ball on bat
In play the pitcher must aim between the

ALL TIME STAR

Playing for the New York Yankees from 1936–51, Joe DiMaggio, nicknamed 'Joltin Joe' hit 361 home runs and set a record in 1941 for getting at least one hit in 56 consecutive games. Off the field he was famously married to Marilyn Monroe from 1954–55.

batter's knees and armpits – the strike zone. After four pitches outside the zone, providing the batter has not swung at any of them, the batter is allowed to go to first base. If three balls are pitched within the zone but the batter hits none of them or hits one or more outside the foul line, then the rule 'three strikes and you're out' applies. When the ball is hit inside the field the batter begins to run, but will be adjudged out if the ball is caught by a fielder before it touches the ground, or if a fielder who has the ball tags (touches) him or first base before he reaches it.

Because only one batter can occupy a base at any time, it is possible for batters to be tagged out as they go round the diamond. A batter hitting well enough to complete the entire diamond and return to the home base is said to have completed a home run. A home run is also automatically scored if the ball is hit beyond the grassline.

The Word Series

Throughout the season baseball is played in two leagues, the American League (AL) and the National League (NL). The World Series, inaugurated in 1903, and also known as the Fall Classic is played between the top four teams in each league, culminating in a seven-game series between the two leagues. The New York Yankees, once the New York Highlanders, clearly top the chart of top five winners:

Team	Series wins	Series played	Year last won	Year last played
New York Yankees (AL)	27	40	2009	2009
St Louis Cardinals (NL)	11	19	2011	2013
Oakland Athletics (AL)	9	14	1989	1990
San Francisco Giants (NL)	8	20	2014	2014
Boston Red Sox (AL)	8	12	2013	2013

Home runs

Making 650 or more home runs is a huge baseball achievement surpassed by only a few:

Player	Team/s	Home runs	Year achieved
Barry Lamar Bonds	Pittsburgh Pirates/San Francisco Giants	762	2007
Hank ('Hammer') Aaron	Milwaukee Braves/Atlanta Braves/Milwaukee Brewers	755	1976
George Herman ('Babe') Ruth	Boston Red Sox/New York Yankees/ Boston Braves	714	1935
Alex ('A-Rod') Rodriguez	Seattle Mariners/Texas Rangers/New York Yankees	696	2016
Willy Mays	New York/San Francisco Giants/New York Mets	660	1973

CHANCING YOUR LUCK

IN MANY GAMES, INCLUDING DICE GAMES, IT CAN BE HELPFUL TO KNOW YOUR CHANCES OF WINNING. AND IT IS EVEN MORE IMPORTANT IF YOU ARE BETTING ON A RESULT.

When you toss a coin, what is the probability of getting heads or tails? Most people know that it is 50 per cent or one in two, written as ½. But suppose you toss the coin half a dozen times, what is the probability of it coming up tails each time? The answer to this is 1 in 2^6 or 1 in 64. Some people assert that on the 'law of averages' the next toss will be heads, but this just isn't true. Each toss of the coin is an independent event for which the odds are 50 per cent or ½ no matter how many events or 'trials' have gone before.

Despite the fact that, in the long term with hundreds of tosses being made, the results would show close to 50 per cent heads and 50 per cent tails, the odds of throwing 3 heads and 3 tails in 6 trials are actually only $^{20}\!/_{64}$, or simplifying the figure, $^{5}\!/_{16}$ or 37½ per cent.

Calculating the odds

Surprisingly, there is an easy way of working out the odds just by adding up numbers in the following way. It was devised by the French mathematician Blaise Pascal (1623–62), who played a large role in the development of probability theory.

Start like this:

$$
\begin{array}{ccccccc}
 & & & 1 & & 1 & & & \text{sum} = 2 = 2 \\
 & & 1 & & 2 & & 1 & & \text{sum} = 4 = 2^2 \\
 & 1 & & 3 & & 3 & & 1 & \text{sum} = 8 = 2^3 \\
1 & & 4 & & 6 & & 4 & & 1 \quad \text{sum} = 16 = 2^4 \\
\end{array}
$$

```
          1    1          sum = 2 =2
        1   2   1         sum = 4 = 2²
      1   3   3   1       sum = 8 = 2³
    1   4   6   4   1     sum = 16 = 2⁴
  1   5  10  10   5   1   sum = 32 = 2⁵
1   6  15  20  15   6   1 sum = 64 = 2⁶
```

This may be used when predicting the results of coin tossing. Using the last line, it is possible to deduce that if you toss the coin 6 times, there are $64 = 2^6$ outcomes.

Probability of 6 heads = $^{1}\!/_{64}$

Probability of 5 heads and 1 tails = $^{6}\!/_{64}$

Probability of 4 heads and 2 tails = $^{15}\!/_{64}$

Probability of 3 heads and 3 tails = $^{20}\!/_{64}$ (as mentioned above)

Probability of 2 heads and 4 tails = $^{15}\!/_{64}$

Probability of 1 heads and 5 tails = $^{6}\!/_{64}$

Probability of 6 tails = $^{1}\!/_{64}$

Again, you need to remember that each toss is independent, so that tossing four heads in a row in no way increases or decreases the probability of a tail in the 5th throw, or another head.

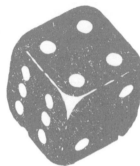

Lucky dice

In games in which dice are thrown to generate an element of chance, very often two of the most common six-sided dice are thrown, producing a score between 2 and 12, with 7 as the most likely result.

The chances are as follows:

2	**1 in 36 (equal least likely)**
3	**2 in 36**
4	**3 in 36**
5	**4 in 36**
6	**5 in 36**
7	**6 in 36 (most likely result)**
8	**5 in 36**
9	**4 in 36**
10	**3 in 36**
11	**2 in 36**
12	**1 in 36 (equal least likely)**

Total	**36 in 36.**

If the two numbers in the total are not the same, then there has been a mistake – or the dice have been loaded. The total probability of all the events is one, because $\frac{36}{36} = 1$.

Very sophisticated games have been developed from the simple act of throwing a pair of six-sided dice on multiple occasions, including backgammon and craps.

Dice may also be made out of the other regular polyhedra (see Throwing dice). The tetrahedral (or 4-sided) does not really 'roll' very well, but dice made from octahedra (8-sided) dodecahedra (12-sided) and icosahedra (20-sided) work really well and allow an equal probability if sides are marked as 1 to 8, 1 to 12, and 1 to 20 respectively. Of course the sides need not be marked with sequential numbers that can produce results that are interestingly asymmetrical.

Chances at bridge

In the game of contract bridge, popular worldwide, each of four players are dealt 13 cards each from the pack of 52. To win at bridge it is helpful to have good luck in the deal. However it is essential to count the cards as they are played, because you can make key assumptions based on the cards in your own hand. So if you have 5 spades, for example, the other 8 in the suit will most likely be divided among the other three

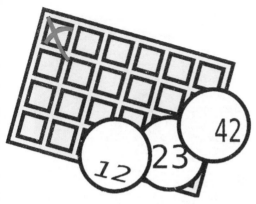

players as 2, 2 and 4 or 1, 3 and 4. Least likely are 0, 0 and 8 and 1, 1 and 6.

It is possible to find charts of probabilities for all the possible hands in bridge. The hand you are most likely to be dealt will consist of two suits of four cards each, one suit of three cards and a fourth suit of two cards (a doubleton).

A BIG DEAL

It has been calculated that in bridge there are 53.36×10^{28} possible deals, that is 536 followed by 26 more numbers. If each deal occupied just a single square millimetre the answer would be an area more than 100 million times the earth's surface area.

A WINNING TICKET?

The same principle as coin tossing applies to lotteries. For even when a number has not featured in a winning line for months this does not mean that it is any more or less likely to feature in the following draw. When the National Lottery was first introduced to Britain in 1994, the choice was 6 numbers from 1 to 49. The odds of picking the correct 6 can be shown in this little formula called 49 choose 6:

1 in $49!/6! \times 43!$ = 1 in 13,983,816.

So what is this funny exclamation mark? It is simply a notation denoting what is called a 'factorial'. So 6! or factorial 6 is:
$6 \times 5 \times 4 \times 3 \times 2 \times 1 = 720$.
The exclamation mark is most appropriate, because factorials get very big surprisingly quickly!

By 2018 the National Lottery choice had been upped to 6 from numbers 1 to 59. which means that the odds of picking the correct 6 numbers has got a great deal tougher. They are now 1 in 59 choose 6 which is:

1 in $59!/6! \times 53!$ = 1 in 45,057,474

THROWING DICE

NUMBERS FEATURE IN A WHOLE VARIETY OF POPULAR GAMES AND PUZZLES FROM DICE TO SUDOKU, MANY OF THEM DATING BACK MANY MILLENNIA.

Six sides

Made from bones – often the knuckles – dice have been played for at least 5,000 years, or so the archaeological evidence from sites in Sumeria, India and Pakistan suggests. The standard dice or die is a cube bearing one to six dots, arranged so that the sum of opposite sides adds up to seven. Legend has it that during a prolonged famine in the 5th century BC, when the subjects of the king of Lydia were only permitted to eat on alternate days, dice games were invented to help pass the time.

Both Greeks and Romans were avid dice players, with a triple six (the chance of which is 1 in 216) being the throw to aim for. Not only were some Romans professionals, but the Emperor Claudius even wrote a book on the subject in the 1st century AD. Roman dice came in two sizes, the *tali* were large dice with numbers on only four sides, these being one, three, four and six. On the smaller *tesserae* numbers were arranged in the now standard pattern.

As well as bone, dice have been made from a whole range of materials, including lead, crystal, glass, ivory, silver, gold, wood and marble. Today's versions are commonly made from plastic, by injection moulding and mechanically polished with an abrasive. Casino dice are often made to appear transparent with the pips drilled on in a separate process. They also have a number stamped on them to prevent them being substituted by would-be cheats.

DICE OF MANY SHAPES

As early as the 2nd century 20-sided dice were being made and dice of many shapes are popular with gamers. Some popular shapes include:

Tetrahedron – each of the four faces bears three numbers. When the dice is thrown three faces are visible. The winning numbers are the ones that appear upright.

Octahedron – eight triangular faces, with the sum of opposite faces adding up to nine.

Pentagonal trapezohedron – 10 kite-shaped faces bearing the digits zero to nine.

Dodecahedron – 12 faces, each a regular pentagon and with the values of opposite faces adding up to 13.

Icosahedron – 20 faces each an equilateral triangle. When numbered 1 to 20 the opposite sides add up to 21.

There are all manner of ways in which dice can be unfairly loaded to make them fall a particular way. These include adding weight, removing material from the corners and making the cube so that its faces are not quite exact squares.

Backgammon

Dice for the two-player game of backgammon are usually smaller than the casino variety and have rounded corners to facilitate play. The game is believed to have originated in Mesopotamia (now Iraq) some 5,000 years ago, using dice made from human bones. The Romans were the first to make it truly popular with their version known as *Duodecum Scripta et Tabulae* or simple Tables. Many Roman villas, including those preserved at Pompeii, depict the game being played, often with participants in various states of undress.

In a game of backgammon, which demands a combination of strategy and fortune, each player has 15 pieces, which they move between 24 triangles or points depending on the outcome of rolling a pair of dice. The aim is to be the first to move all 15 off the board, or 'bear off'. With each dice roll players must not only move pieces to their own advantage but anticipate the moves of their opponents. During the game, stakes can be raised by playing a doubling cube.

The game of craps

In the dice game known as craps players bet on the outcome of rolling a pair of dice either once or in a sequence. Craps may have been played by the Romans but the modern version is thought to derive from the game hazard invented during the Crusades by Sir William of Tyre and his knights. It was much later brought to New Orleans in the early 19th century by one Bernard Xavier Philippe de Marigny de Mandeville, the son of wealthy Louisiana landowners returning from London. It was supposedly named from a mispronunciation of 'crabs' the London term for the losing numbers two and three.

Originally scorned by the respectable, craps became a popular street game and migrated to casinos only in the 1930s. The modern version of the game was the brainchild of the American dice maker John H. Winn.

Craps moved from the street to the casino but exploded massively in popularity during World War II when young men of all classes were called up to serve in the military. It was simple to play on just a blanket or any flat surface.

PLAYING DOMINOES

WINNING AT DOMINOES IS ALL TO DO WITH THE NUMBER OF PIPS – THE SPOTS MARKED ON EACH END OF THE RECTANGULAR PLAYING PIECES WHOSE NICKNAMES INCLUDE BONES, CARDS, TILES, STONES, TICKETS, CHIPS AND SPINNERS.

Dominoes was certainly enjoyed in China in the Song dynasty (1232–98), and the oldest 32-piece sets were made to represent each possible face of two thrown dice (see Thowing dice). How the modern game played in Italy in the 18th century relates to the original remains a mystery, although some scholars believe that it reached Europe with missionaries. Traditionally domino pieces, which are plain on the reverse side, were made of ivory with black pips of ebony with white pips. Each piece is twice as long as it is wide.

Each set of today's set of 28 dominoes contains tiles from 0-0 to 6-6 (doubles) with all the possible number combinations in between. So-called double nine sets of 55 pieces are also available. Starting with 7 tiles for each player, the aim of the game is to lay tiles that match with those of your opponent and to be the first to lay all of your tiles. If a player can't go, then they must take a tile from those remaining (left face down). Should no player be able to finish, then the one with the lowest number of pips in their remaining tiles is the victor.

ALL IN A NAME

The name domino almost certainly comes from the French word for a woollen hood worn by priests and from the Latin *dominus* meaning master or lord. There may also be a link to the carnival costume of black hood and white mask traditionally worn in Venice.

SOLVING THE SQUARE

ALTHOUGH MANY ARE CENTURIES OLD, NUMBER PUZZLES BASED AROUND THE SQUARE CONTINUE TO FASCINATE AND ENTERTAIN US TODAY.

All 'square' games consist of a large square containing a number of smaller squares or cells. Oldest of all is the magic square in which the numbers in every row and column of cells – all of which are different – add up to the same total. A simple 3 × 3 square, with every row and column adding up to 15, looks like this:

2	7	6
9	5	1
4	3	8

Invented by the Chinese in the 3rd millennium BCE, the magic square is linked with the Emperor Yu, who used as his inspiration a turtle with an unusual pattern on its shell. The magic square he created, which he dubbed the Lo Shu, came to be regarded with awe. It was believed to link heaven and earth, be a talisman for good fortune, aid childbirth and even give power to alchemists. It certainly appears in the *I Ching*, the ancient Chinese book of divination and in *Da Dai Liji*, a book of rites dating to the Zou Dynasty and later in literature across Europe.

Spreading the magic

By medieval times, magic squares were known and created in India, the middle east, and north Africa, although for Arab scholars such as Abu'l-Wafa al-Buzjani

their appeal was purely mathematical. As they became more well known, 'prescriptions' for creating them burgeoned. The Indian mathematician Narayana Pandit declared in 1356 that creating them could destroy the egos of bad mathematicians and give good ones pleasure.

Magic squares were not only a pastime for mathematicians but engaged monks in places such as Germany from where this 12th century solution presented the square as this charming puzzle: 'There were three brothers at Cologne who had nine casks of wine. The first cask contained 1 bucket, the second 2, the third 3, the fourth 4, the fifth 5, the sixth 6, the seventh 7, the eighth 8, the ninth 9. Divide the wine equally among these three without breaking any casks.' The answer is that each monk will get 15 buckets of wine.

SOME FAMOUS MAGIC SQUARES

In his well-known engraving 'Melencholia 1' of 1514, the German painter and engraver Albrecht Durer included a 4 × 4 magic square, revealing the magic number of 34 in this pattern:

16	3	2	13
5	10	11	8
9	6	7	12
4	15	14	1

The reason behind his choice remains a mystery but scholars have suggested that it points to a belief that an unknown power could cure the subject's condition, possibly by using alchemy to supply riches.

Although not a perfect example, because it repeats the numbers 10 and 14, the magic square depicted on the Passion façade of the Sagrada Familia church in Barcelona is notable because each row and column adds up to 33, the age of Jesus at the time of his crucifixion.

The American politician and polymath Benjamin Franklin discovered magic squares in a French book by Bernard Frenicle de Bessy, loaned to him by a Mr Logan and published the first of his own invention in 1767. His most famous creation is this 8 × 8 magic square in which every row and column adds up to 260. What is more, every half row and half column adds up to 130 and the four corners plus the middle make 260.

14	3	62	51	46	35	30	19
52	61	4	13	20	29	36	45
11	6	59	54	43	38	27	22
53	60	5	12	21	28	37	44
55	58	7	10	23	26	39	42
9	8	57	56	41	40	25	24
50	63	2	15	18	31	34	47
16	1	64	49	48	33	32	17

Benjamin Franklin's Magic Square

In modern times, the famous Indian mathematician Srinivasa Ramanujan created a series of magic squares in which the first row 22, 12, 18, 87 were the numbers of his birth date, 22 December 1887. He was not able, of course, to include or even predict his death date which would have been 26, 4, 19, 20.

Sudoku: the daily workout

Contrary to popular belief, the Sudoku has modern, not ancient origins, appearing first in the French newspaper *Le Siècle* in the late 19th century. Originally based on the magic square it very quickly became refined and by 6 July, 1895, when the rival paper *La France* published its first version, its construction was very similar to the one that taxes us today.

Haward Garns, a retired architect from Connersville Indiana is credited with inventing the modern Sudoku first published in 1979 by Dell Magazines. Each 3 × 3 subsquare in the puzzle must contain the number 1 to 9 and there must be no repeats of numbers in any full row or column. The puzzle did not get its name until after 1984 when it was introduced in Japanese paper *Monthly Nikolist* with a name translating as 'digits must be single'.

Eventually Sudoku reached Britain where it was an instant hit, beginning with puzzles published in *The Times* (originally as Su Doku) from 2 November, 2004. The catalyst in this advance was the Hong Kong judge Wayne Gould who, after seeing a partially completed puzzle in a Japanese bookshop developed a

The first ever live TV Suduko programme, *Sudoku Live*, hosted by Carol Vorderman was aired by Sky One on 1 July, 2005. Nine teams of nine contestants competed to solve the puzzle. The winner, Phil Kollin of Winchester, netted more than £23,000.

computer programme that could turn out unique puzzles at speed.

While a daily Sudoku puzzle is a great workout for the brain, it is not, although it involves numbers, a strictly mathematical puzzle. Because its solution (unlike the magic square) depends solely on group theory rather than arithmetic it could work just as well with a series of nine letters or symbols.

Variation on a theme

Invented in 2004 by the Japanese maths teacher Tetsuya Miyamoto, the KenKen puzzle, whose name comes from the Japanese term for cleverness, was devised specifically as a brain training exercise. As in Sudoku the aim is to fill a grid with digits so that no digit appears more than once in any row or column, but in addition the grid contains clearly identified groups of cells or cages, each with an instruction as to how the numbers must be manipulated (by addition, subtraction, multiplication or division) to produce the target indicated.

5	3			7				
6			1	9	5			
	9	8					6	
8				6				3
4			8		3			1
7				2				6
	6					2	8	
			4	1	9			5
				8			7	9

Sudoku puzzle

So, in a cage of two cells with the instruction 11+ the only two numbers that can satisfy the instruction are 5 and 6. Other cages create more choice, so that 6× could be created by 6 and 1 or 2 and 3.

KenKen followed Suodku into the pages of *The Times* in March 2008 after the chess grand master Dr David Levy showed the puzzles to Michael Harvey, one of the newspaper's editors. Because it combines arithmetic and logic, KenKen is widely used as an educational tool and is now used by more than 30,000 teachers in the USA on a regular basis.

KenKen puzzle

The 15 puzzle

Also known as the Gem Puzzle, Boss Puzzle, Game of Fifteen and the Mystic Square, the 15 puzzle is a Victorian invention played by children ever since – at least until superseded by computer puzzles. Essentially the puzzle consists of a series of randomly arranged plastic squares within a frame, leaving one square empty so that the others are free to move. The aim of the game is to shuffle the squares so that they finally appear in order – from 1 to 8 in a 3 × 3 puzzle and from 1 to 15 in a 4 × 4 design.

The puzzle was invented in 1874 by Noyes Palmer Chapman, a New York postmaster. The original game, with no frame contained elements of the magic square since the aim was to arrange the squares in rows, each adding up to 34. By 1897, thanks to Chapman's son Frank, the game was being manufactured by students in the American School for the Deaf in Hartford Connecticut. Only three years later the game had become a craze not only in North America, but all over Europe.

Writing in the 1914 *Cyclopedia of Puzzles* the chess player and puzzle master Sam Loyd claimed to be the inventor of the 15 Puzzle. Perhaps aiming to endorse his claim Loyd offered a prize of $1,000 for anyone who could solve the puzzle but reverse the numbers 14 and 15. This is actually impossible!

INDEX

prices 61
prime numbers 46, 53, 61–2, 69–71, 78, 113
    EMIRPS 70
    Mersenne 70–1
    new 70–1
    Olympic Gold 69
    pattern of 71
    seven 32
    sexy 70
    three 21
    two 19
Prinsengracht 263 123
probability theory 189–91
proverbs 144, 146
Ptolemy 90, 110
punched cards 16
Pythagoras 10, 13, 17, 19, 29, 38, 59, 62–3, 72–5, 80, 165
Pythagoreans 21, 23–4, 26, 29, 32, 44, 57, 63

quadrillion 66

Ramanujan, Srinivasa 61, 196
Rann, John `Sixteen String' 53
rational numbers 75, 76
records 166
red blood cells 114–15
reindeer, Santa's 39
Rhind Papyrus 37
Richter Scale 44, 87
roads 84, 127–9
Romans 13–14, 17, 20, 23, 34, 47, 53, 60, 94–5, 98, 101, 104, 106, 108, 192–3
Rowling, JK 155
rugby football 174–6

Sagan's number 67
Sayers, Dorothy L. 150
science fiction 151–2
Science of Numbers 62
Scottish tradition 41, 54, 56
Scoville heat units 135
Se7en 158
seas 86
seconds 110

Seed of Life, The 33
Sellar, W.C. 152
senses 118
seven 32–7, 63, 65, 146–8, 171–2
Seven Brides for Seven Brothers 158
Seven Samurai 158
Seven Wonders of the World 35–6
Seven Year Itch, The 158
sexual reproduction 119
Shakespeare, William 32, 40, 48, 107, 167–9
Shannon, Charles 16
shapes, making with numbers 72–3
Shrubsole, Anya 182
Sibbitz, George 16
sight 118
Sikhs 27
single-celled organisms 113
six 29–31, 63, 65
six degrees of separation 30
Six Degrees of Separation (film) 157
Sixth Sense, The 157
skeleton 114
skin 117, 118
small numbers 68
smell, sense of 118
Snallgaster 19
sneezing 58
snooker 185–6
Snow White 34
snowflakes 31
solstices 86, 89, 90
Solzhenitsyn, Alexander 150–1
song 161–3
sonnets 168–9
Sosigenes 106
South Pole 89
sperm 119
spinal cord 116–17
spirals, Fibonacci 78–80
sport 144, 170–88
square numbers 72–3
square puzzles 195–8
standard deviation 83
Star of David 29
Stymphalian Birds 51

OTHER GREAT TITLES FROM RYDON PUBLISHING

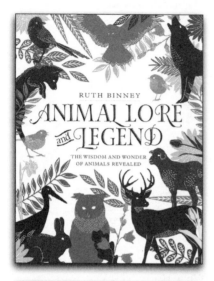

Animal Lore and Legend
Ruth Binney
ISBN: 978-1-910821-15-2

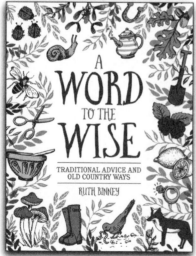

A Word to the Wise
Ruth Binney
ISBN: 978-1-910821-11-4

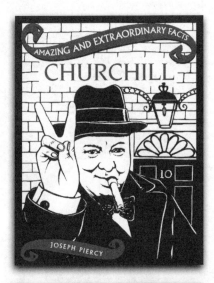

Amazing and Extraordinary Facts
Churchill
Joseph Piercy
ISBN-13: 978-1-910821-07-7

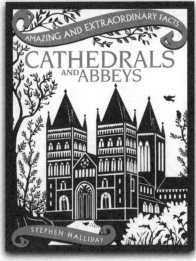

Amazing and Extraordinary Facts
Cathedrals and Abbeys
Stephen Halliday
ISBN-13: 978-1-910821-04-6

ABOUT THE AUTHOR

Since childhood Ruth Binney has been fascinated with the world and the way it works. She holds a degree in Natural Sciences from Cambridge University and has been involved in countless publications during her career as an editor. She is the author of many successful natural history and nostalgia titles, including *Animal Lore and Legend* (2017), *A Word to the Wise* (2016), *Plant Lore and Legend* (2016), and *The English Countryside*. She lives in Yeovil, Somerset.

www.ruthbinney.com